W9-BVO-609

ORTHO® ALL ABOUT

Citrus
& Subtropical Fruits

Meredith® Books
Des Moines, Iowa

Ortho All About Citrus & Subtropical Fruits
Editor: Denny Schrock
Contributing Editor: Lance Walheim
Contributing Writers: Paul Moore, Claude Sweet
Contributing Photographers: Ed Gohlich, Douglas Hetherington
Copy Chief: Terri Fredrickson
Copy Editor: Kevin Cox
Publishing Operations Manager: Karen Schirm
Senior Editor, Asset and Information Management: Phillip Morgan
Edit and Design Production Coordinator: Mary Lee Gavin
Art and Editorial Sourcing Coordinator: Jackie Swartz
Editorial Assistant: Susan Ferguson
Book Production Managers: Pam Kvitne, Marjorie J. Schenkelberg, Mark Weaver
Imaging Center Operator: Brian Frank
Contributing Copy Editor: Susan Lang
Contributing Consultants: Mary Lu Arpaia, Gary Bender, Robert Bergh, James Beutel, Rob Brokaw, John Brown, Tony Brown, Carl Campbell, Bob Chambers, C. Collins, Tom Cooper, R.E. Coronel, Norman Ellstrand, George Emerich, Jim Gilbert, Tom Gleason, Francis Gouin, Rudy Haluza, Gene Joyner, Ron Kadish, Robert Kurle, Richard Langdon, Kirk Larson, Brian Lievens, Paul Lyrene, Michael McConkey, Louis Migley, Dan Milbocker, John Moore, Jim Neitzel, Dorothy Nichols, Robert Norton, Jan Pirzio-Biroli, Gayther Plummer, John Riley, Chris Rollins, Kay Ryego, Dale Sato, C.C. Schaller, Art Schroeder, James B. Shanks, Wayne Sherman, Bob Smith, Steven Spangler, Jerry Staedeli, W.B. Storey, Jack Swords, J.L. Tayor, Paul Thompson, Ronald Tukey, William F. Whitman, Horace Whittaker, Kathleen Williams, William Wiltbank
Contributing Technical Proofreaders: Jonathan H. Crane, Tom Del Hotal, Dave Slaybaugh, Claude Sweet
Contributing Proofreaders: Ellen Bingham, Stacie Gaylor, Elise Marton
Contributing Map Illustrator: Jana Fothergill
Contributing Indexer: Ellen Sherron
Other Contributors: Janet Anderson, Muriel & Ben DeKoning, Encanto Farms Nursery, Four Winds Growers, Dan Kinnard & Eloise Lau, Art & Dottie Logan, Leo Manuel, Monrovia Nursery, Ben Poirier, Primavera Orchards, Quail Botanical Gardens, Chris Rollins, University of California Lindcove Research Station, Mongi Zekri

Additional Editorial Contributions from Abramowitz Creative Studios
Publishing Director: Tim Abramowitz
Illustrator: Kelly Bailey

Additional Editorial Contributions from Art Rep Services
Director: Chip Nadeau
Designer: lk Design
Illustrator: Shawn Wallace

Meredith® Books
Editor in Chief: Gregory H. Kayko
Executive Director, Design: Matt Strelecki
Managing Editor: Amy Tincher-Durik
Executive Editor: Benjamin W. Allen
Senior Associate Design Director: Tom Wegner
Marketing Product Manager: Brent Wiersma

Executive Director, Marketing and New Business: Kevin Kacere
Director, Marketing and Publicity: Amy Nichols
Executive Director, Sales: Ken Zagor
Director, Operations: George A. Susral
Director, Production: Douglas M. Johnston
Business Director: Janice Croat

Senior Vice President: Karla Jeffries
Vice President and General Manager: Douglas J. Guendel

Meredith Publishing Group
President: Jack Griffin
Executive Vice President: Doug Olson

Meredith Corporation
Chairman of the Board: William T. Kerr
President and Chief Executive Officer: Stephen M. Lacy

In Memoriam: E.T. Meredith III (1933–2003)

Photographers
(Photographers credited may retain copyright © to the listed photographs)
L = Left, R = Right, B = Bottom, T = Top

William D. Adams, 7T, 90L, 104BR; Charles Marden Fitch, 92R, 94BL; Getty Images, Alfrendo Images, 113B; Getty Images, Quentin Bacon/stockfood, 113T; Getty Images, daj/daj, 8; Saxon Holt, 92L, 108TR; Jerry Pavia, 4, 13, 24R, 90R, 93L; Richard Shiell, 108L

All of us at Meredith® Books are dedicated to providing you with the information and ideas you need to enhance your home and garden. We welcome your comments and suggestions about this book. Write to us at:
Meredith Corporation
Meredith Gardening Books
1716 Locust St.
Des Moines, IA 50309-3023

If you would like more information on other Ortho products, call 800/225-2883 or visit us at: www.ortho.com

Note to the Readers: Due to differing conditions, tools, and individual skills, Meredith Corporation assumes no responsibility for any damages, injuries suffered, or losses incurred as a result of following the information published in this book. Before beginning any project, review the instructions carefully, and if any doubts or questions remain, consult local experts or authorities. Because codes and regulations vary greatly, you always should check with authorities to ensure that your project complies with all applicable local codes and regulations. Always read and observe all of the safety precautions provided by manufacturers of any tools, equipment, or supplies, and follow all accepted safety procedures.

CONTENTS

SUBTROPICAL FRUITS

Subtropical fruits may be as familiar as the navel orange or as novel as the cherimoya. Whether borne on trees, shrubs, herbs, or vines, they add richness to the landscape and excitement to the table.

These fruits generate a special kind of delight for gardeners. Mango, papaya, banana, sapote, macadamia, and passionfruit call to mind faraway places and interesting new flavors. Even the familiar orange tree evokes enticing images of sunny days, fragrant blossoms, and swaying palm trees. This romantic appeal is one reason that so many gardeners are planting edible landscapes containing subtropical plants.

Another reason for the increasing interest is that more subtropical fruits have begun to appear in supermarkets in recent years. And if a fruit tastes good from the supermarket, it will be even better if homegrown.

Although most subtropical fruits are usually imported, many others are now cultivated in the United States. As more people grow subtropical fruits, the foundation of experience expands, new techniques develop, and everyone's prospects improve. Today home gardeners from California to Florida are raising subtropical fruits with increasing success.

Gardeners in cold climates can also get in on the fun of growing subtropical plants, many of which will bear fruit in greenhouses—or even outdoors if protected in winter.

◀ Colorful fruits and fragrant flowers make citrus an ideal choice for ornamental edible gardens. In this garden oranges provide shade for Lenten rose and Japanese painted fern.

WHAT ARE SUBTROPICAL FRUITS?

This book introduces new and unusual fruits. Some included here are not truly subtropical. They may be tropical (native to areas close to the equator), and others could be considered temperate (native to areas with very cold winters). But all of them have one thing in common: They can be grown outdoors in mild-winter regions of the United States, which can be broadly described as subtropical. These areas have some of the most desirable climates in the world, but gardeners living in many of them may not be able to grow America's favorite fruits: apples, cherries, peaches, and other plants that require cold winters for fruit production. For these gardeners subtropical fruits are an unusual alternative.

▼ Pineapple, papaya, avocado, mango, guava, strawberry guava, and banana are some of the more widely grown subtropical fruits. Durian (the large fruit at upper center) is grown only in the tropics.

▲ Intensely fragrant kaffir lime is one of the many exotic members of the citrus family.

WHY SUBTROPICAL FRUITS?

▲ **Passionfruit vine bears wonderfully intricate flowers followed by delicious fruits.**

The most obvious reason for growing subtropical fruits is so you can enjoy fresh fruit ripened to perfection. There are some other good reasons for cultivating these plants.

Landscape quality

The tropical landscape is one of the most appealing garden designs. Large bold leaves, fragrant flowers, and brightly colored fruit combine to create a tropical feeling that attracts home gardeners and landscape architects. Many of the subtropical fruits described in this book are among the best plants for creating a tropical ambience. Few plants have the dramatic presence of banana, the year-round appeal of strawberry guava, or the intense color of passionfruit blossoms. Some of the plants have a variety of uses in the landscape—for example, citrus can be pruned as a hedge or espaliered, kiwifruit and passionfruit vines can be trained to cover a fence or arbor, and figs make stunning shade trees. Also many of the plants adapt well to containers.

▶ **'Meyer' lemons are small, compact trees perfect for containers, indoors or out. Like many types of citrus, they can bear fruit and bloom at the same time.**

The challenge

Growing fruit of any kind takes a certain amount of commitment. Fruiting plants in general, whether they are apples, pears, or mangoes, are not usually considered low maintenance. Also the further from ideal the growing conditions are, the more attention the plants need. But that challenge also makes success more rewarding. If you learn what a plant needs, provide the best possible planting site, and make special adjustments to allow the plant to thrive, your success will be more enjoyable.

On the other hand some subtropical fruits are easy to grow in many areas. Citrus, figs, persimmons, and avocados are undemanding plants and, where adapted, provide abundant harvests with a minimum of attention.

Excitement at the table

New flavors and fresh ingredients always make cooking and eating more exciting and enjoyable. Foreign dishes are more authentic and often more delicious when they are made with the same ingredients used by the people who developed them.

Subtropical fruits are versatile and nutritious. Fresh lemons are a necessity for many cooks, and citrus is well known for its vitamin C content, but the more unusual subtropical fruits also have great nutritive and culinary value. Papayas contain an enzyme that is supposed to aid digestion, avocados contain vitamins A through K, and bananas are almost as rich in vitamins B and C as oranges are.

HOW TO USE THIS BOOK

◀ Avocados, oranges, papayas, and bananas are just a few of many delicious choices for subtropical fruit gardens.

Learn how your climate affects the adaptation, growth, and productivity of subtropical fruits. Chapter 2, "Understanding Climate," beginning on page 8, describes aspects of plant adaptation, such as hardiness, as well as heat and humidity requirements. It tells you how to take advantage of your garden's microclimates so your plants will grow and yield bountiful harvests.

The basics of growing the plants are found in Chapter 3, "Caring for Subtropical Fruits," beginning on page 16. Here you'll find the essentials you need to know about soils, planting, watering, fertilizing, pruning, controlling pests and diseases, and propagating.

Chapter 4, "Subtropical Fruits in Containers," beginning on page 32, includes specific suggestions on how gardeners in cold-winter areas can successfully grow the plants indoors in winter and outdoors in summer, or year-round in a greenhouse.

Next familiarize yourself with the most common subtropical fruits. Chapter 5, "Citrus," which begins on page 38, and Chapter 6, "The Best Subtropical Fruits," which begins on page 62, describe each fruit and provide information on such topics as adaptation, propagation, site selection and planting, care, and harvest and storage.

The "Resources" section (page 122) is devoted to helping you find the varieties of subtropical fruits you want and putting you in touch with other people who share your interest. It lists nurseries that specialize in subtropical fruits and organizations dedicated to their culture.

◀ In cold climates overwinter containers of subtropical fruits such as banana in a greenhouse.

UNDERSTANDING CLIMATE

Subtropical fruits can be grown in a variety of climates when given proper care. This chapter describes suitable climates and shows how to modify a garden to provide the best microclimate.

The elements place severe restrictions on plants, and subtropical fruits are no exception. Your grapefruit will be sweet enough to eat only if the tree has absorbed enough sunlight and heat. A kiwifruit vine won't bloom satisfactorily if it doesn't get enough winter chilling. Cherimoya sets more fruit when it flowers in mild, humid weather, but mango must have warm, dry conditions while it is flowering to produce a crop.

Part of the gardener's art is to grow plants in areas where they wouldn't normally flourish. To meet this challenge consider your climate and the needs of the plants you are growing.

▼ **Citrus trees grow best in mild climates where temperatures seldom drop much below freezing.**

CLIMATE VARIABLES

Each plant has a specific set of climatic requirements, which are described in the "Adaptation" section of each plant description in this book. Some requirements affect the survival of the plant; others influence fruit quality and productivity but not necessarily survival.

Cold tolerance

Every plant has a low-temperature limit and will be damaged if exposed to temperatures below that point. For many plants the hardiness limit has been determined, and you can consult the USDA Plant Hardiness Zone Map on this page for a general impression of adaptation. Unfortunately it's not easy to predict the performance of subtropical fruit species on the basis of the map. Many subtropical plants carry their fruit through winter, and others bloom during cold months. Flowers and fruits are almost always less hardy than foliage and will usually be damaged if temperatures stay below freezing for very long. Consult individual plant listings for specific temperature tolerances.

On the brighter side soil insulates roots against cold temperatures. So even if the top of a plant is killed, new shoots may sprout from the roots the following spring. Grafted trees will have to be regrafted, but seedling-grown plants will continue to produce the same fruit as before.

There are many ways you can protect plants from the cold, as shown on page 14. Plants that are hardened off and are growing at a reduced rate or are completely dormant due to exposure to cold are hardier than those that are still growing actively. To encourage fall hardiness avoid feeding tender plants any nitrogen fertilizer from mid- to late summer. Feeding can encourage new growth that may be damaged by the first frost of the season.

Heat requirement

Next to damage from cold temperatures, insufficient warmth is the greatest limiting factor in growing subtropical fruits. Without enough heat bananas will hang on the plant without ripening and citrus will fail to sweeten properly. Passionfruit flowers will not develop into fruit. Papaya plants will rot at the base. Each plant is affected differently, but the usual result of cool summer conditions is failure of the fruit to ripen properly.

Some fruits are damaged by too much heat. For example, 'Washington' navel orange and cherimoya will not set fruit in the heat of the desert Southwest. Many fruits can be ruined by sunburn in hot, arid climates.

▼ The USDA Plant Hardiness Zone Map classifies plants by the coldest temperature and zone they can endure. To find your hardiness zone, note the approximate location of your community on the map, then match the color band marking that area to the key.

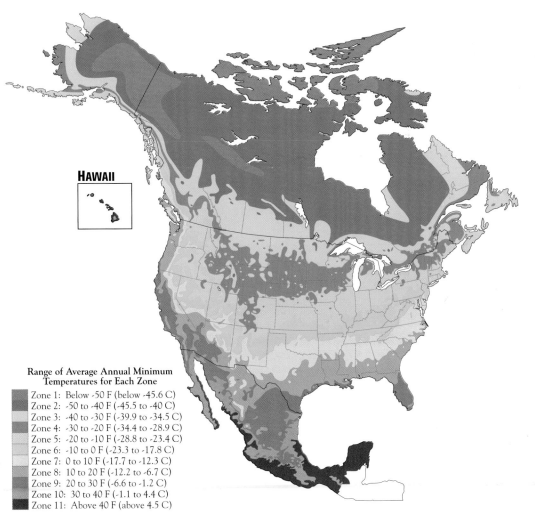

HAWAII

Range of Average Annual Minimum Temperatures for Each Zone

Zone 1: Below -50 F (below -45.6 C)
Zone 2: -50 to -40 F (-45.5 to -40 C)
Zone 3: -40 to -30 F (-39.9 to -34.5 C)
Zone 4: -30 to -20 F (-34.4 to -28.9 C)
Zone 5: -20 to -10 F (-28.8 to -23.4 C)
Zone 6: -10 to 0 F (-23.3 to -17.8 C)
Zone 7: 0 to 10 F (-17.7 to -12.3 C)
Zone 8: 10 to 20 F (-12.2 to -6.7 C)
Zone 9: 20 to 30 F (-6.6 to -1.2 C)
Zone 10: 30 to 40 F (-1.1 to 4.4 C)
Zone 11: Above 40 F (above 4.5 C)

▶ Large leaves and huge fruit clusters make bananas one of the most tropical plants in appearance, but unless protected from wind, foliage tears and tatters.

Rainfall and humidity

Atmospheric moisture affects plants in many ways. Abundant rainfall and high humidity ease your watering chores but greatly increase the chances of fungal and bacterial diseases. Rain can also interfere with pollination. On the other hand lack of humidity may dry out cherimoya flowers and prevent self-pollination.

You can influence humidity by adjusting your watering schedule and method to weather conditions. To minimize diseases in humid areas, avoid wetting the foliage and water in the morning so the soil surface will have a chance to dry before nightfall. When humidity is low sprinkler irrigation can temporarily raise humidity.

Sunlight

Almost all the fruits described in this book must be grown in full sun. Sunlight supplies the plant with energy to produce the sugars that will eventually make your fruit sweet and delicious. In a desert climate, however, many plants benefit from partial shade during the hottest part of the day. Too much sunlight can also present a problem for recently pruned plants. To prevent sunburn paint exposed branches and the trunk with water-base white paint (diluted with an equal amount of water) or commercially available tree paint.

Wind

Strong winds increase drought stress, break fruit-laden branches, and tear large leaves. The best way to protect wind-sensitive species is to plant them downwind of other, tougher species. Windbreaks are usually effective for a distance 10 times their height. Walls and solid fences aggravate wind problems, causing strong turbulence on both sides of the structure.

Chilling requirements

Several subtropical fruits, including fig, kiwifruit, and persimmon, require exposure to a certain number of hours of temperatures between 32° and 45°F in winter. Insufficient chilling causes plants to leaf out slowly and bloom irregularly, which can lead to sunburn and a general decline in vigor and yield. To expose a plant to maximum chilling, plant it in a low spot or area adjacent to a wall or fence at the bottom of a slope where cool air collects.

Varieties within a species often have different chilling requirements. Low-chill varieties are the only types of some fruits that can be grown in mild-winter climates.

CLIMATE REGIONS

The climate of an area is influenced by a complex interaction of many factors, including weather patterns, longitude, latitude, and topography. Also a large body of water will moderate local climate. Generally, however, four main climates—tropical, semitropical, subtropical, and temperate—are suitable for growing subtropical fruits.

Tropical

Consistency is the key feature. Because a tropical climate has no distinct seasons, abundant rainfall, high humidity, and warm temperatures occur throughout the year. Under such conditions many plants act in a surprising way. Some grow actively every month, often producing several crops. Oranges, for example, may flower four or five times in a year. You might think this would be a boon for tropical orange growers, but oranges do another odd thing in tropical areas—they stay green. Citrus develops its characteristic rind color only when the temperature drops below 45°F for an extended period, which it seldom does in tropical regions. This means an orange tree may hold green fruit in four or five different stages of ripeness. Picking ripe fruit becomes a problem.

Many of the fruits described in this book are native to tropical areas of the world. If you live in a tropical area such as Hawaii, keeping in mind the consistent characteristics of the climates should help you make these plants more at home in your garden.

▲ The maroon foliage of 'Red Malaysian' guava adds a colorful splash to tropical gardens.

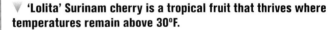

▽ 'Lolita' Surinam cherry is a tropical fruit that thrives where temperatures remain above 30°F.

◁ Trying to grow tropicals in semitropical regions may result in winter dieback. This longan suffered severe winter injury, but is regrowing from the roots.

Semitropical

South Florida and areas along the Gulf Coast have a typical semitropical climate. Although humidity and annual rainfall are high, as they are in tropical areas, a semitropical region has recognizable seasons. Summers are hot, and winters are generally warm with occasional cold spells. During some winters cold arctic air flows down from the north, often devastating tender plants.

Subtropical

A subtropical region is dramatically different from a semitropical one. The humidity may be very low in inland areas. Rainfall is often concentrated in the winter months and in some areas amounts to less than 10 inches a year.

Although the low-elevation regions of California and Arizona are subtropical, there is great variation within these areas. Southern California and inland desert areas are hot and dry with relatively warm winters. Farther north winters are colder and rainier and frosts are common. Frost-free areas near the coast are generally cool throughout the year because of their proximity to the Pacific Ocean. The inland valleys are quite hot in summer.

Temperate

Found throughout most of the United States, areas with temperate climates generally have well-defined seasons, but the length of the seasons and their extremes differ according to latitude and local geography. Growing many of the plants in this book successfully means moving them to a protected area in winter. (See Chapter 4, "Subtropical Fruits in Containers," beginning on page 32.) However, several of the hardier fruits, such as persimmon, fig, and kiwifruit, can be grown outdoors year-round in milder temperate areas.

▲ Green-and-yellow striped 'Panachee' figs are among the hardiest fruits described in this book. With some winter protection they can be grown outdoors year-round in Zone 6.

◄ The olive tree in the foreground and the 'Dancy' tangerine in the background provide welcome shade and tasty fruit for the owners of this walled patio area.

MICROCLIMATES

The climates described on pages 11–12 are those of towns, counties, regions, or even states. There is little anyone can do to change them. However, you can alter microclimates, the distinct climates around your home that are slightly different from the general climate of your area.

Solar energy, the prime mover of all weather, is an impressive force. You can take advantage of the different ways this energy is absorbed and reflected to modify the microclimates of your garden to suit the needs of your plants.

Radiation principles

The heat of sunlight may be either desirable or undesirable, depending on where you live, the season, and the plants you would like to grow.

Various things happen as light and heat come from the sun to your garden. Part of the energy is reflected into space by clouds, part of it is scattered and diffused as it strikes small particles in the earth's atmosphere, and part of it is absorbed by carbon dioxide, water vapor, and ozone in the atmosphere. The remainder, approximately one-fifth, penetrates directly through the atmosphere to the earth's surface, where it is absorbed or reflected.

As a result the plants in your yard may receive solar energy as reflected radiation from atmospheric particles, as reflected radiation from materials on or near the earth's surface, or as direct radiation from the sun.

▓ **Absorption, radiation, and reflection**
At night the earth radiates some of the heat it absorbed during the day. Materials vary in the amount of radiation they store, depending on their composition. Loose organic mulches, like bark chips, store much less heat than a dense inorganic one such as gravel.

Because light-colored surfaces reflect more than dark ones, you can use the color of a material as a microclimatic control. Dark surfaces absorb more heat that is released later. Light-colored objects reflect more heat and light. By planting next to a light-colored wall, you can maximize the amount of heat a plant receives during the day. Conversely you can locate a plant next to a dark wall to keep it warmer at night.

▓ **Exposure** At most latitudes in the Northern Hemisphere, the south side of a home receives the most sun year-round. The east side basks in morning light, the west side receives the hottest afternoon sun, and the north side is shaded much of the time. Of course the light intensity changes with the seasons, but in general if you want maximum heat, plant on the south or west side of your home.

△ **Growing citrus near a south-facing wall can hasten ripening and provide frost protection from heat absorbed by the wall during sunny periods.**

Frost protection

You can successfully protect any tender plant against cold if you are willing to try hard enough. Many gardeners plant in containers and move their fruit trees indoors during winter (see page 35). Others construct plastic covers to trap heat radiating from the soil or bury their plants in protective mulches. But in many areas the most important thing is to recognize cold spots in the garden and select the warmest possible planting site.

Two types of cold weather can damage plants: radiation frost and advective freeze. Radiation frost occurs on cool, clear, still nights when plants and the objects around them radiate heat to the sky. Water may condense on the leaves if the humidity is high enough, but the plants can be damaged even if no visible frost condenses. To avoid radiation frost damage, plant sensitive species next to a south-facing wall that will store heat during the day and release it at night. A roof overhang above the plants will reduce the amount of heat radiated to the sky and provide additional protection. Canvas and plastic covers will also protect plants from radiation frost damage. The heat radiated from the soil will help keep the plant warm. Also avoid planting in low spots, where cold air settles.

An advective freeze occurs over a wide area as a result of an influx of arctic air; such freezes are common in Florida and Texas. The techniques used to protect against radiation frosts will also protect plants in advective freezes.

▶ **You can wrap young citrus trees with a cylinder of wire covered with microfoam insulation to provide frost protection. Fill the cylinder with loose straw stuffed around the trunk and branches.**

▶ **Wrap young trees to protect the trunk from sunburn and to insulate the bud union from cold damage in winter.**

▲ **A wood frame covered in plastic will provide a few degrees of frost protection. For added warmth hang a lamp from the frame.**

▲ **Stone mulch placed at the base of a tree's trunk absorbs heat during the day and releases it at night to prevent frost damage.**

◄ Organic mulch protects roots of young citrus trees. You can also mound it around the trunk to provide some insulation to the bud union.

◄ Citrus grown in containers can easily be taken into protected areas during cold spells.

▲ Ice from sprinklers insulates citrus foliage from the coldest temperatures. Keep the sprinklers running until the air temperature rises enough for the ice to melt on its own.

▼ Antitranspirant spray offers several degrees of frost protection. Repeat applications will be necessary during wet weather.

◄ Freeze-damaged lemons dry out on the inside and develop a pithy texture.

◄ Tender new growth, such as that on this lemon tree, is most susceptible to frost damage.

CARING FOR SUBTROPICAL FRUITS

Like other plants, subtropical fruits thrive when given proper care. In this section you'll find the basics you need to know about soils, planting, watering, fertilizing, pruning, propagating, and controlling pests. The plants described in this book originate from all over the world and as a group have cultural requirements that cover the spectrum of horticultural practices. Thus it is important to consider all the requirements of a species before you plant.

▶ **Inspect plants regularly for insects and diseases. Treat them with appropriate controls before a problem becomes serious.**

CHOOSING PLANTS AT THE NURSERY

Most subtropical plants are sold in the containers in which they were grown. An exception to this general practice are standard-size citrus trees, which may be grown in fields, then dug up and placed in containers (usually tall, narrow plastic containers called sleeves) for sale in nurseries. Field-grown plants have usually been pruned to compensate for roots lost during digging and do not have the full appearance that plants grown in a container have. Both types do well once in the ground, as long as they have not been in their nursery pots too long.

Look for healthy specimens that show signs of active growth. Avoid plants with signs of stagnation, such as yellow or poorly colored leaves, dead branches, or large, circling roots near the soil surface. Container plants can be planted anytime as long as they are kept moist prior to and after planting.

Some plants, such as persimmon and kiwifruit, are sold bare root. Usually deciduous, bare-root plants are dug up while dormant and sold with their roots packed in sawdust. Some mail-order nurseries also sell evergreen plants such as citrus bare root in order to minimize shipping costs. When selecting a bare-root plant, look for a well-formed system with roots extending in all directions. Avoid plants with damaged or dry roots. Keep bare-root plants cool and moist. Plant them as soon as possible.

Some mail-order citrus nurseries (see page 122) ship trees bare root. Plant such trees immediately upon receiving them.

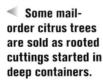

Retail nurseries and garden centers sell citrus and many other subtropical fruit trees grown in containers of various sizes.

Some mail-order citrus trees are sold as rooted cuttings started in deep containers.

UNDERSTANDING SOIL

> **Rich loam soil holds moisture and nutrients well and is well-aerated and well-drained.**

For healthy growth plants need three things from soil: moisture, nutrients, and air. Most clay soils absorb water slowly and drain poorly. As a result these soils are poorly aerated. If water fills air spaces for too long, the roots will die, causing the top to die as well. You know you have a clay soil if it is rock hard when dry and sticky when wet. When you squeeze a wet handful, it stays slippery and compressed when released. Clay has a high nutrient-holding capacity.

Sandy soils absorb water rapidly and drain rapidly, leaving plenty of air but little water. Because sandy soils hold nutrients poorly, plants growing in them need to be fertilized more frequently. You can tell you have a sandy soil if the texture is gritty. When you grab a handful and squeeze, it easily breaks apart when released.

Most soils have properties between those of sand and clay. These soils, called loams, vary greatly in texture and structure but often have a desirable combination of good aeration and high water- and nutrient-holding capacity.

To improve excessively sandy or clayey soils add organic matter. Compost and other organic materials loosen and aerate clay soils and help sandy soils hold moisture and nutrients. Sand is not a good amendment for clay soils; the particles of sand aggregate with the clay and turn the soil into something resembling concrete.

Before planting in large beds, blend 4 to 6 inches of organic matter into the top 12 inches of soil. Avoid amending backfill soil only. Keep the soil under the canopy covered with mulch (see page 23). An organic mulch will slowly decompose and continue to improve the soil.

If your soil has a hardpan or other impervious layer below the topsoil, organic matter will not improve the drainage. In such cases it's best to plant in containers or raised beds.

Soil pH

The pH of a soil is a measure of its acidity or alkalinity. The pH scale runs from 0 (extremely acidic) to 14 (extremely alkaline). The middle of the scale (7) is the neutral point.

Soil pH is important because it affects the availability of essential nutrients. For instance, plants adapted to acidic soils often show signs of iron chlorosis (yellowing of foliage) when grown in alkaline soils. Most subtropical fruits grow best in slightly acidic soils, but many tolerate slightly alkaline conditions, especially if they are given foliar feedings of micronutrients.

Testing the pH of a soil is easy; you can use an inexpensive kit, available at most nurseries and scientific supply houses. Most cooperative extension services also perform soil tests or refer you to someone who can. You usually have to pay a fee for this test, but you get more data than you do with a kit, including such helpful information as soil texture and nutrient content.

Adjusting soil pH is relatively easy, although it can take quite a bit of time. If your soil is too acidic, a common condition in areas with abundant rainfall, the most reliable cure is to add ground limestone to the soil. If alkalinity is the problem, add sulfur, aluminum sulfate, or ferrous sulfate, or fertilize with an ammonium fertilizer such as ammonium phosphate.

These soil amendments are available in most nurseries. Application rates vary according to the pH and soil type, so ask your nursery staff or your cooperative extension agent for exact rates.

Soil salts

Most subtropical plants are sensitive to salts. Salty soils are most commonly found in areas with low annual rainfall and alkaline soil, such as portions of the desert Southwest. Salts may originate in irrigation water or fertilizer residues. In areas that receive ample rainfall, salts are naturally leached through the root zone.

The first symptom of salt damage is slow growth. In severe cases the edges of the leaves become burned. If you suspect that high levels of salt are damaging your plants, leach the soil by watering deeply every third or fourth irrigation. Well-drained soil is necessary for successful leaching. If your soil is both salty and poorly drained, consider growing your subtropical fruits in raised beds or containers.

PLANTING

The best time to plant subtropical fruits is in spring, after the danger of frost has passed, so the plants can become established before winter.

PLANTING CONTAINER-GROWN PLANTS

1 Dig a hole at least twice as wide as the root ball and to a depth that allows the top of the root ball to sit slightly above the grade of the surrounding soil.

2 Gently remove the root ball from the container.

3 Loosen matted or circling roots by raking through them with fingers, or cut the roots with a sharp knife.

4 Position the tree in the hole and check the depth of the root ball by placing the shovel handle across the hole. Adjust the depth of the hole if necessary.

5 Fill the hole with existing backfill soil.

6 Create a watering basin over the top of the root ball by mounding soil in a ring.

7 Water the root zone thoroughly. Fill the moat created by the ring of soil.

PLANTING *(continued)*

PLANTING BARE-ROOT PLANTS

1 Dig a hole at least twice as wide as the root ball and to a depth that allows the plant to sit slightly above its original planting depth (look for a color change along the trunk).

2 Prune away damaged or tightly wound roots.

3 Spread out the roots in the bottom of the hole.

4 Work the backfill soil between and around the roots, firming it as you go.

5 Create a watering basin over the top of the root ball; water thoroughly.

WATERING

How often to water and how much water to apply depend on a number of factors. By understanding how these factors affect your specific situation, you'll be able to develop a watering schedule that suits the needs of your plants.

Soil type Plants grown in sandy soils need to be watered more often than those grown in clay soils.

Weather If you live in a rainy area you won't have to water as often as someone in a dry climate. It's also true that plants need more water in hot weather than in cool weather. Because wind dries out plants more rapidly than still air does, plantings in windy sites need more frequent watering.

Type of plant Fast-growing, shallow-rooted plants with large leaves such as banana need much more water than slow-growing, deep-rooted plants such as persimmon. Because their root systems are limited, young plants need more frequent watering than established plants.

Water deeply Apply enough water to wet the entire root zone. For most trees this is at least 24 inches deep. Larger trees may need to be watered to a depth of 4 feet or more. Deep watering encourages deep rooting and extends the period the plant can go between waterings.

A soil tube or soil auger is a useful tool for determining how deep water has penetrated and how much moisture is in the soil between irrigations. Use the tool to remove a core of soil from the root zone and examine it for moisture. In loose soils you can push a stiff piece of wire or a steel rod into the soil after watering. It will move easily through moist soil and become difficult to push when it reaches dry soil.

Target water to the roots Use basins, furrows, or drip irrigation to direct water to the roots. If you use a basin adjust its size as the plant grows. During a wet season make small breaks in the walls of the basin to allow excess water to drain away.

Let the soil partially dry Allowing the soil to dry somewhat between irrigations promotes healthy root growth and helps prevent soilborne diseases. Even though many fruit trees are deep rooted, most roots are in the top 8 to 12 inches of soil. To determine when to water, examine the soil often. A good guideline is to water when the top 6 to 8 inches of soil are dry.

Mulch Use mulch to conserve soil moisture. Spread the material about 3 to 4 inches thick, but keep it away from the trunk. (See page 23 for more about mulches.)

Water application

You can apply water in several ways: in basins, by sprinklers, or by a drip system.

Basins Soil basins simplify watering and are easy to construct. Once you know how deep 1 inch of water will penetrate, adjust the height of the basin walls or the number of times you fill the basin. In sandy soil 1 inch of water will usually penetrate to a depth of 12 inches, but in clay soil it may reach only 3 to 6 inches deep.

Sprinklers Match the application rate of the sprinkler to the soil's ability to absorb water. Sprinklers that apply water too fast can cause erosion and wasteful runoff. Take care to position a sprinkler so it doesn't wet the tree trunk. Sprinklers have one important advantage: They can also be used for frost protection (see page 15).

Drip systems Drip emitters discharge water at very low rates, usually between ½ and 1 gallon per hour, to a precise area. Evaporation and waste are minimized. A young tree needs at least four emitters evenly distributed beneath its canopy.

Perhaps a better solution is to use a modified drip system called trickle irrigation. In this method low-volume (5 to 50 gallons per hour), low-pressure minisprinklers, which emit a fanlike spray with a radius of 3 feet or more, substitute for emitters. The larger coverage area wets the root zone more evenly and the larger orifices of the minisprinklers are less susceptible to clogging, which is a constant problem with drip emitters. With either type of system make certain that the entire root zone is wet after irrigating. Use a soil probe to check depth of water penetration.

◀ **Trickle irrigation applies a gentle spray of water to the root zone near a young citrus tree. Avoid wetting the trunk. As the tree grows add emitters near the outside of the dripline (extent of branch spread). Space emitters 1–3 feet apart. Check their output at least annually to make certain they are functioning properly.**

FERTILIZING

Most fruit trees grown commercially have been studied carefully to determine which nutrients they need for maximum fruit quality and quantity. If you grow citrus, persimmon, or fig, your cooperative extension service can supply you with a specific fertilization program developed for your area. The encyclopedia descriptions of these fruits include specific information on when and how much fertilizer to apply. Unfortunately few other subtropical fruits have been so carefully studied in North America.

To fertilize properly you need to know how fertilizers affect plants. Each essential element plays a specific role in plant growth. Nitrogen stimulates leafy growth, often at the expense of flower production. It must be applied regularly because it is quickly leached through the soil. Phosphorus and potassium promote flowering and fruiting. Because they are less mobile, they don't need to be applied as frequently as nitrogen.

Applying too much fertilizer can be more damaging than applying too little. Fertilizers are salts that leave acidic or alkaline residues; excessive use of fertilizer may burn plants and alter the soil pH.

Soils and fertilization

Soil and climate directly influence the way you fertilize. Sandy soils are less fertile than clay soils, and problems caused by poor fertilizing practices can develop more rapidly in sandy soils.

Soils in areas with high annual rainfall, such as Florida, are generally well leached and low in fertility. These soils are usually acidic and are deficient in many nutrients. They are generally low in nitrogen, iron, phosphorus, boron, zinc, manganese, copper, and molybdenum.

▶ Yellowing between leaf veins on new growth usually means that the plant is suffering from an iron deficiency.

◀ General leaf yellowing, especially in older parts of the plant, signifies a likely nitrogen deficiency.

Soils in arid regions, such as Southern California and Arizona, receive low annual rainfall. Little leaching takes place, so these soils are alkaline and most essential nutrients are available in sufficient amounts. In general nitrogen, iron, and zinc may be the only nutrients required.

A soil test is the best way to determine exactly which nutrients are available in your soil. Contact your local cooperative extension service for information on soil laboratories in your area.

Reading fertilizer labels

Fertilizers are labeled according to how much nitrogen (N), phosphorus (P), and potassium (K)—the three major nutrients—they contain. The percentages may change, but they are always listed in this order: N, P, K. This listing, or analysis, reveals the amount of a nutrient by weight. For example, a 5-pound box of 5-10-10 fertilizer contains 5 percent nitrogen (or 0.25 pound of actual nitrogen, which is 5 percent of 5 pounds), 10 percent phosphate (a form of phosphorus), and 10 percent potash (a form of potassium). It helps to know the amount of nitrogen in the box or bag since most recommendations are given in pounds of actual nitrogen per plant or given area.

The analysis also tells the relative proportions of N, P, and K. For example,

▼ Improper fertilization affects foliage color, plant vigor, fruit size, and fruit quality.

a ratio of 2-1-1 (such as 10-5-5 or 20-10-10) indicates that there is twice as much nitrogen as phosphate and potash. Choose the fertilizer that contains the best proportions of N, P, and K for your site.

▲ Miracle-Gro Shake 'n Feed Continuous Release Citrus, Avocado & Mango Plant Food is formulated with magnesium, sulfur, iron, manganese, and zinc to improve common nutrient deficiencies on these crops.

Types of fertilizer

Dry fertilizers are available in soluble and slow-release formulations. Since slow-release fertilizers are only slightly soluble in water, they release nutrients over time—from six weeks to two years, depending on the fertilizer.

The most common type of slow-release fertilizer, urea-formaldehyde, is broken down by bacteria into a soluble form available to plants. Other slow-release fertilizers are coated to reduce their solubility, or formulated with slightly soluble materials that become available without bacterial activity.

The amount of slow-release nitrogen in a fertilizer is shown on the label as a part of the nitrogen analysis. It is called water-insoluble nitrogen and is shown as a percentage of the total fertilizer. For example, a fertilizer that is 10 percent nitrogen might contain 8 percent water-soluble nitrogen and 2 percent water-insoluble nitrogen.

Liquid fertilizers are often preferred for container plants because they dissolve and distribute nutrients evenly throughout the root ball. However, container plants need frequent watering, which leaches nutrients from the root ball. Consequently they need to be fertilized more often. For more information on growing subtopical fruits in containers, see page 32.

Organic fertilizers are often expensive, but their residues may last a long time in the soil, improving its structure. Whenever using bulk manures, make sure they have been fully composted.

Micronutrients

Many complete fertilizers include micronutrients, but sometimes plants need micronutrients only. In these cases apply a foliar spray of chelated micronutrients to fully expanded leaves in early spring.

Fertilizer rates

It's safest to apply fertilizers three or four times during the growing season, beginning in late winter and ending in late summer. Fertilizing after late summer can delay dormancy in subtropical plants and increase the chance of damage from sudden cold weather in the fall.

Light feeders include avocado, feijoa, fig, loquat, and persimmon. They need little or no fertilizer. For other subtropical fruits apply 1 to 2 tablespoons of a complete fertilizer three or four times during their first two growing seasons. From the third to the eighth year, gradually increase the feedings from ¼ to 1 pound of actual nitrogen per year. From the ninth year onward, give plants between 1 and 1½ pounds of actual nitrogen per year.

MULCHING

Useful in gardens generally, mulches are particularly beneficial to subtropical plants. Mulch materials include black plastic, ground bark, cocoa bean hulls, decomposed sawdust, composted grass clippings, gravel, and leaves. When properly applied, mulch improves the garden for plants and people by:
- conserving soil moisture
- protecting soil from being compacted by foot traffic
- reducing soil erosion
- moderating soil temperature
- inhibiting weed growth
- helping to improve the soil structure and fertility if the mulch is organic

In addition some mulches reflect extra heat into a tree to ripen fruit in cooler climates.

On the downside, plants in mulched areas may be more susceptible to frost damage because less heat is absorbed by the soil and radiated at night. For the best frost protection, rake the mulch away to expose the ground around the plant during cold spells or use a gravel mulch, which stores heat during the day and releases it at night. When severe temperatures are predicted, leaving a mulch in place can protect plant roots, allowing them to resprout if the top is damaged or killed. If a tree has been grafted, mounding mulch or soil over the graft union can protect both the roots and the fruiting variety.

Never pile mulch against a tree trunk or plant stem, because it can cause rot. Keep it at least 6 inches away. An exception to this rule is in cold climates, where mulch is piled extra high to protect the trunk. Plastic mulches can be used to warm soil and prevent weeds, but unless they are perforated they can restrict water penetration and root growth. Landscape fabric, available in nurseries and garden centers, allows for water penetration and restricts weeds. As a mulch it is often a better choice than plastic.

PRUNING

▶ Heading cuts are made along the length of a branch, just above a node.

◀ Regrowth from a heading cut often results in two or more shoots developing below the cut.

▶ Thinning cuts remove an entire branch at its origin.

◀ Regrowth from a thinning cut usually results in only one new shoot from the area of the cut.

▶ Thin out closely spaced branches and those that form a narrow crotch angle with the main stem or trunk.

◀ Wide-angle branches support the weight of developing fruits.

Unlike most temperate fruit trees, which must be pruned carefully and frequently for best fruit production, most subtropical fruit species require no drastic annual pruning. Kiwifruit and passionfruit are two exceptions; prune them regularly to promote flowering, to restrain vigorous growth, and to keep the fruit within easy reach.

Even though pruning may not always be necessary, in many cases you will want to prune your plants to control their size, to make them more attractive, or to stimulate new growth and heavier yields. The two types of pruning cuts you can make are thinning and heading.

Thinning cuts remove branches or limbs where they join the rest of the plant, resulting in a more open plant. By thinning main shoots back to shorter side branches, you can decrease the size of a plant without destroying its natural character.

Heading cuts remove the terminal or top of a branch, resulting in vigorous growth from dormant buds just below the cut and a denser, more compact plant. Shearing to form a hedge is a type of heading.

Both thinning and heading control the size of a plant, but thinning usually produces a healthier, more attractive plant.

Some subtropical fruits, such as citrus, fig, and persimmon, can be trained as informal espaliers. An espalier is a plant trained in a flat, vertical plane, usually against a fence, wall, or trellis. Frequent pruning and tying keep the plant flat and productive from top to bottom. Espaliers are particularly effective in areas where space is limited. Formal designs, which have a recognizable geometric pattern to the branches, are often used for apples and pears but are not practical with most subtropical fruits. An informal espalier often ends up looking like a hedge, although it is usually more open.

▲ 'Meyer' lemons can be sheared to create a compact, fruitful hedge. In this garden they are growing in containers to create the effect.

CONTROLLING PESTS AND DISEASES

Most plants, when properly cared for, will resist attacks from insects and diseases. Many pesticides have been approved for use on commercially important subtropical fruits such as citrus and avocado, but other, less common fruits are rarely listed on chemical labels. The best advice for insect and disease control is to prevent problems by following good cultural practices. Drought-stressed, improperly planted, or overfertilized plants are more susceptible to pest and disease problems than vigorously growing plants.

If your plant becomes infested with insects or infected by a disease, use only a chemical approved for that specific plant and follow label directions precisely. Pay particular attention to how close to harvest a spray can be safely applied. Pest control regulations vary from state to state; if you have questions, consult your cooperative extension service.

Listed below are some of the pests and diseases that may trouble subtropical plants and recommendations for control. If a chemical control is mentioned, it does not mean it can be used on all subtropical fruits. Check the label first. Both the pest and the plant being sprayed must be listed on the label for it to be used legally. However, some pesticides list simply "fruit trees" or "fruit" on the label. Although these can be used on some subtropical fruits, proceed with caution; test the material on a portion of the plant several days to a week before using it on the entire plant. Some materials may burn, damage, or even kill subtropical fruits.

Insects

Aphids Small, soft-bodied insects that feed on plant sap, aphids may be yellow, green, red, purple, brown, or black and are usually clustered on plant leaves, stem tips, and flowers. Some aphids are covered with a white waxy coating.

Aphids distort the parts of the plant they feed on and in severe infestations stunt the whole plant. They produce honeydew, a clear, shiny, sticky fluid that coats plant parts and attracts ants. Sooty mold, a black fungus, forms in the honeydew and can turn leaves black. In heavy infestations honeydew can drip from plants, staining pavement and anything else underneath the plants, and sooty mold may cover the surface of the leaves.

The easiest method of controlling

▲ **Citrus aphids usually feed on tender new growth at the stem tips.**

▲ **The citrus orangedog caterpillar is one of many caterpillars that may feed on the foliage of subtropical fruits.**

aphids is to knock them off the plant with a hard spray of slightly soapy water. Lightweight horticultural oil (summer oil) and neem oil are also effective. However, to control aphids you also may have to control any ants present. Ants reestablish aphid colonies and protect them from beneficial insects in order to harvest the honeydew produced by aphids. To control ants, treat the base and trunk of the plant with an appropriate insecticide or apply a sticky barrier around the trunk to prevent the ants from climbing into the plant. Products containing suitable sticky materials to trap ants are sold in nurseries and garden centers.

Caterpillars The larvae of moths and butterflies, caterpillars include such pests as tent caterpillars and leaf rollers. The insects may be smooth, hairy, or covered with spines, and they may feed on leaves, stems, flowers, or fruit.

Bacillus thuringensis (Bt), a biological control, is effective on young caterpillars as is spinosad, another organic control. Ortho Malathion Plus is another option for controlling caterpillars.

Mealybugs Oval insects that cluster in white, cottony masses on stems and leaves, mealybugs—like aphids—suck plant juices. Infested plant parts may be distorted, yellowed, and stunted. Honeydew may cover plant parts and attract ants. Lightweight horticultural oil, insecticidal soap, and neem oil are effective controls, as is Ortho Malathion Plus.

▓ **Mites** These tiny pests are related to spiders. In fact some mite species are commonly called spider mites; they produce webbing that covers the undersides of infested leaves and other plant parts. Feeding by mites causes leaves to become stippled, discolored, and yellow, and

eventually the leaves may die. Mites thrive on water-stressed, dusty plants. The best way to prevent mite problems is to water properly and occasionally spray the plants with water to keep them clean. Lightweight horticultural oil, insecticidal soap, or Ortho Malathion Plus are effective mite controls.

▓ **Nematodes** Microscopic worms that live in the soil and infest plant roots, nematodes usually stunt a plant and may predispose it to infection by diseases or infestation by other pests. In severe cases nematodes can kill a plant.

Some types of nematodes produce small nodules or bulges on the plant roots, but most of the time it's hard to tell if your plant has a nematode problem. If the plants are cared for properly, most will continue to be productive. If you think nematodes are causing serious problems, consult your local cooperative extension service about beneficial nematodes or soil solarization.

▓ **Scale insects** Resembling small fish scales stuck to the plant, these insects may be brown, reddish, or gray and may be covered with a white, waxy material. Adult scale are immobile and feed on the plant's sap. Young scale have no shell and move around on the plant.

Foliage infested with scale turns yellow and may die. In severe infestations the insects may entirely cover the trunk and branches. Like other sucking insects, some scale insects produce honeydew, a sticky, clear, shiny material that attracts ants and promotes sooty mold.

The protective shells on adult scale make them difficult to control. The insects are easiest to manage when young, in the crawler stage; use lightweight horticultural oil (summer oil) or Ortho Malathion Plus. California red scale is controlled in commercial citrus groves by releasing the parasitic wasp, *Aphytis melinus*. Controlling scale also means controlling ants. See the section on aphids on page 25.

▲ **Spider mites usually feed on leaf undersides.**

▲ **Avocado mealybug adults have a waxy, grayish white coating.**

▲ **California red scale can feed directly on lemon fruits.**

▲ **Scale insects may vary in size and stage of development.**

▲ **Thrips cause curling and distortion of citrus foliage.**

▲ **Snails can cause serious damage to citrus foliage.**

▓ **Slugs and snails** These pests feed on flowers, young shoots, leaves, and fruits of many subtropical fruit species. They avoid direct sun and dry places, hiding during the day in damp, protected spots.

Baits containing iron phosphate or metaldehyde (Ortho Bug-Geta Snail & Slug Killer) are recommended for use on many tropical fruit trees. You can also keep slugs and snails under control by cleaning up the debris in which they hide during the day. To reduce snail problems on citrus, prune the lower branches so they don't hang down to the ground, and place a band of copper foil around the base of the trunk (snails and slugs won't cross copper because they receive an electrical shock when they do so). In some parts of Southern California, predatory decollate snails, which are available in nurseries there, are released to control common brown snails.

■ **Thrips** Tiny, slender insects, thrips infest the flowers, leaves, fruits, and shoots of many kinds of plants, which they damage by rasping the plant tissue and then sucking the released sap. Thrips distort flower petals and leaves. Damaged leaves may be flecked or streaked with yellow, or they may have silvery undersides dotted with shiny black spots. Insecticidal soap, spinosad, and Ortho Malathion Plus help control thrips, but since crops are rarely seriously damaged, many citrus growers prefer not to treat at all and let native beneficial insects provide control.

Diseases

The most common diseases of subtropical fruit are encouraged by poorly drained soil or excess water around the trunk of the plant. Trunk canker, foot rot, and root rot can quickly kill plants and are difficult to control once they have taken hold. Watering properly, planting in well-drained soil, keeping wet soil and mulches away from the trunk, and breaking watering basins in rainy seasons so excess water can drain away are the best preventive measures. Various fruit rots and foliage diseases also cause problems in humid climates. The fungicide chlorothalonil (Ortho Garden Disease Control) is registered for disease control on some fruits. Other controls vary depending on the area; consult your local extension service.

■ **Leaf spot** Anthracnose, leaf spot, and powdery mildew are usually caused by fungi. In many cases they do not seriously damage the plant, but some will defoliate a plant, causing it to decline and eventually die. Leaf-spotting fungi are most active in mild, damp weather. To control mild infections simply pick off the damaged leaves. If the infection becomes serious, spray with a copper fungicide or another appropriately labeled fungicide.

■ **Fire blight** This bacterial disease infects subtropical plants in the rose family, such as loquat. It is spread by contaminated water splashing onto flowers, pollinating insects, and pruning shears. Fire blight symptoms are unmistakable: The tips of branches are blackened and appear to be

▲ **Powdery mildew is a grayish fungus that can attack mango.**

▲ **Sooty mold indicates that insects are feeding on the plant.**

▲ **Fire blight on loquat shows up as sudden browning and dieback.**

▲ **These figs have been damaged by birds. Protect them with a net.**

burned (hence the name fire blight).

There are no cures for the disease, but you may reduce the severity of the infection by spraying the plant several times with streptomycin or a copper spray while it is blooming. Stop the disease from spreading by pruning out infected branches as soon as you see them; cut several inches below the blackened area. Sterilize your shears after each cut by dipping them in rubbing alcohol or a 10 percent solution of chlorine bleach (1 part household bleach to 9 parts water).

Animal pests

Many bird species feed on ripening fruit. The most effective way to deter them is to temporarily cover the plants with protective netting. Mice, voles, and rabbits will eat the bark of young trees. If enough bark is removed to girdle the tree, the roots will die and the shoots will wither. Protect the trunk with hardware cloth or wire mesh. Check the material occasionally to make sure it doesn't slip or girdle the tree. Gophers can kill fruit trees by feeding on plant roots. Control them by lining planting holes with gopher cages fashioned from hardware cloth or by trapping them.

PROPAGATING SUBTROPICAL FRUITS

▶ **Citrus is easy to grow from seed, but seedlings may take years to fruit. In addition the fruits that develop may bear little resemblance to the parent from which the seed came.**

The more you experiment with growing subtropical fruits, the more you'll want to propagate your own plants. Nurseries will not always be the best source of the varieties you desire, so you will inevitably have to start plants from seed or propagate a friend's plant by rooting cuttings, budding, grafting, or some other technique. Grafting and budding can also be used to restore the top of a tree that has been killed below the bud union or to place pollinating limbs in trees that require cross-pollination.

The five basic methods of propagating plants are germinating seeds, rooting cuttings, grafting and budding, dividing plants, and air layering. The success of each method varies among species and even among varieties of the same species.

Growing plants from seed

Most subtropical fruits can be propagated from seeds. Exceptions include banana, pineapple, and seedless types of citrus and persimmon. Because fruit quality and other characteristics of most plants are variable in seed-grown plants, however, this propagation method is usually used only to produce rootstocks that will later be grafted or budded to selected varieties.

Papaya, passionfruit, and tree tomato are examples of fruits that can be started from seed. You can take the seeds from supermarket fruit, germinate them, and expect the resulting plants to produce good fruit. With other types of subtropical fruits, you never know what you'll get, and the plants will probably take years to bear fruit.

Germination requirements differ for each plant, but in general seeds need warm temperatures, moisture, and a suitable medium to germinate. Seeds from most subtropical fruits germinate best if the soil temperature stays between 70° and 80°F. To accomplish this you'll need to supply bottom heat to keep the soil warm. There are many products on the market designed to heat a flat of soil.

Seeds from some deciduous fruits, including kiwifruit, persimmon, and pomegranate, require a long period of cold storage (stratification) at temperatures between 32° and 40°F before they germinate. Such chilling simulates the natural winter conditions necessary to break dormancy. To stratify seeds place them in a plastic bag filled with damp peat

SIDE GRAFTING

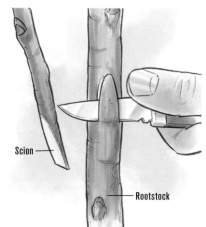

Scion

Rootstock

▲ Make a tapered cut about 1 inch long on both sides of the scion and into the rootstock.

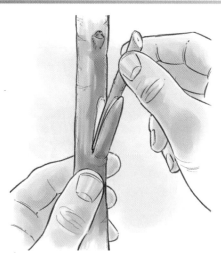

▲ Insert the scion into the rootstock, making certain that the cambium layers of the stock and the scion are in direct contact with each other.

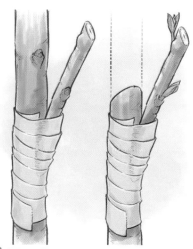

▲ Wrap the graft and wait for new growth to begin. After 6 to 8 weeks remove the top of the rootstock. Allow the grafted shoot to grow.

WHIP GRAFTING

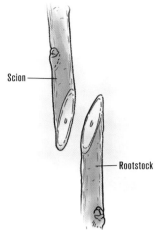

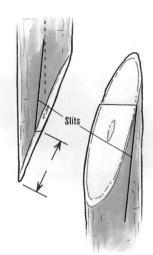

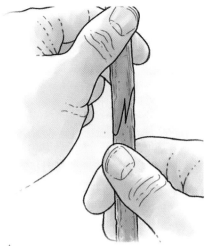

▲ Cut the scion and rootstock at the same angle to ensure a close match.

▲ Make slits in the cut ends, starting a third of the way from the point and angling toward the center.

▲ Join the pieces together so they lock in place with cambium layers in contact. Wrap with grafting tape.

moss and store them for several months in the vegetable compartment of your refrigerator. Keep kiwifruit seeds in the fruit during the stratification process.

Germinate seeds in a nursery flat filled with sterile potting soil. Most seeds should be planted just below the soil surface. Covering the flat with clear plastic or a piece of glass maintains the high humidity necessary for germination. But be careful: Too much moisture encourages soil diseases that can attack seeds and seedlings. Germination time varies by type of plant.

Most subtropical fruit seeds remain viable for several months, but some seeds, such as those of citrus, lychee, and mango, are quite perishable once they have been separated from the fruit. Mango seeds are enclosed in a husk that must be removed before planting. Also the seeds will not

be viable if the fruit has been stored at a temperature below 55°F.

Grafting and budding

These techniques involve fusing a piece of stem or a single bud of a selected variety (scion) with a rootstock. For the procedure to be successful, the cambium (a thin layer of growing tissue beneath the bark) of the scion and the rootstock must be in contact. Formation of callus (a hard, white tissue) at the union between the scion and the rootstock is a sign that the bud or graft has taken.

Evergreen plants are usually grafted in spring. Graft deciduous plants while they are dormant or early in the growing season. Each piece of scion must have at least one well-developed but dormant bud. High

T-BUDDING

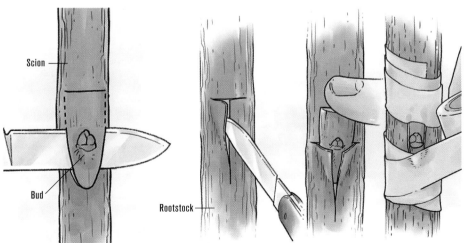

▲ Remove a bud by cutting from ½ inch below to ¾ inch above it.

▲ Make a T-shape cut in the rootstock; separate the flaps. Insert the bud into the cut until its top is even with the top of the "T"; secure with tape.

▲ Remove the top of the rootstock after the bud has begun to grow, usually in 6 to 8 weeks.

CHIP BUDDING

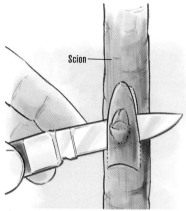

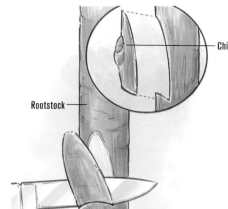

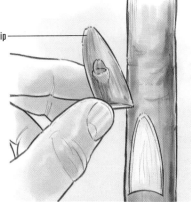

▲ Cut a chip containing a bud from a piece of scion wood.

▲ Cut an identical-shape chip from the rootstock.

▲ Insert the scion bud into the rootstock so that the cambium layers touch each other.

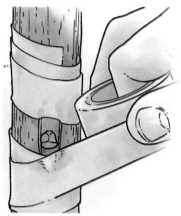

▲ Tape the chip tightly, leaving the bud exposed.

▲ After the bud begins to grow—in about 6 to 8 weeks—cut off the main shoot of the rootstock.

Although a variety of specialized grafting tools are available, you can make do with a sharp pocketknife, grafting tape, a good pair of pruning shears, and a can of commercially available grafting sealer. You may also need a small cleaver, a hammer and nails, and a pruning saw for grafting large limbs.

Rooting cuttings

In this form of propagation, you remove short pieces of stem and stimulate them to form roots at the basal end. There are three types of cuttings, which differ only in the maturity of the growth being propagated. A cutting taken from new growth at the tip of a branch is referred to as a softwood cutting; one taken from growth that is six to eight weeks old is described as a semihardwood cutting; and a section taken from the oldest growth of the current or past season (if the plant is dormant) is called a hardwood cutting.

Subtropical fruits that can be propagated by cuttings may form roots on softwood cuttings but not hardwood cuttings, or vice versa. So it's important to take cuttings at the right time and from the right portion of the plant. To stimulate root development use a rooting hormone according to the label directions. Retain as many leaves on the cutting as is practical, and maintain high humidity. A 60:40 mix of perlite and peat moss is a popular rooting medium for subtropical fruit species. Keep the temperature of the medium between 75° and 85°F with a heating system designed for plant propagation.

humidity and warm temperatures, such as those found in greenhouse conditions, favor success.

Tightly wrap mango scion wood with a piece of wire several weeks prior to cutting it from the mother tree. This girdling forces the scion wood to store food and stimulates development of latent buds.

Budding is probably the easiest grafting method. It allows a large number of plants to be propagated from a small amount of scion wood and is also suitable for larger trunks and stems. Budding can be done whenever the bark is slipping (when it separates easily from the cambium). This is usually in spring, when the plants are actively growing, but budding can also be done in summer and fall. The most common forms of budding are illustrated on page 29 and above.

SOFTWOOD CUTTINGS

▲ Make the cutting about 6 to 8 inches long at the stem tip.

▲ Remove leaves from the lower 3 inches of the stem.

▲ Strip a slice of bark from each side of the base of the cutting.

▲ Dip the base of the cutting into rooting hormone.

▲ Place the cutting in well-drained rooting medium.

▲ Cover the cutting with plastic to maintain high humidity.

Dividing plants

Bananas cannot be propagated by rooting cuttings, grafting, or air layering, but they do produce suckers or offshoots identical to the mother plant, which can be detached and rooted. Take as large a piece of the mother root as possible when removing the offshoot; small shoots may not have enough stored food to establish new roots. Remove one-third to one-half of the foliage from the division, tie the remaining leaves together, and plant the division in warm soil. Maintain high humidity to keep the shoots from drying out.

Air layering

Many fruiting plants are propagated by air layering. This method calls for removing a ring of bark from the parent plant, treating the wound with rooting hormone, and forcing new roots to form on the shoot. After the shoot is rooted, remove it from the parent and plant it. See below for step-by-step photographs of how to do this technique on citrus.

AIR LAYERING

▲ Remove an inch-wide ring of bark and scrape the cambium layer.

▲ Dust the scraped cambium with rooting hormone to stimulate new root growth.

▲ Cover the ring with slightly moist sphagnum moss and wrap with plastic.

▲ When roots fill the sphagnum moss bundle, cut the shoot and plant it.

SUBTROPICAL FRUITS IN CONTAINERS

Container plantings offer the gardener versatility and opportunity because many plants that would not survive if planted in the garden will thrive in pots—indoors and out.

Growing subtropical fruits in containers solves many otherwise insurmountable problems of soil, site, and climate. If the soil in your yard is poorly drained, you can fill a container with a soil mix that will be properly aerated, hold moisture, and drain well. You may not have a place in your yard with sunlight suitable for year-round cultivation of a particular species, but if the plants are in containers you can move them around as the weather dictates. But most of all, if you live in a cold climate, you can enjoy many of the species in this book that would not survive a winter outdoors. Containers are wonderfully mobile; you can move them indoors or to a greenhouse for protection from the coldest winters and then back outdoors when the weather is favorable for growth.

Growing subtropical fruits in handsome pots that complement their distinctive habits lets you enjoy the plants close up. Move them to center stage to show them off when they're in fruit or flower, then shuttle them back to their ideal growing areas whenever you want to.

◀ **Growing citrus trees in containers brings their beauty and fragrance up close to small spaces such as patios and decks.**

CONTAINER SOILS

The perfect container soil combines optimal aeration and drainage with good moisture retention and the ability to hold nutrients. It should also be lightweight so that the containers can be moved easily. Garden soils are not good container soils because they rarely drain properly, are usually too heavy, and often contain disease organisms.

Instead use one of the many potting soils specifically formulated for growing plants in containers. Consider using a mix that has moisture-control amendments and controlled-release fertilizer already mixed in such as Miracle-Gro Moisture Control Potting Mix. These features cut down on the frequency of watering and feeding that you'll need to do.

If you prefer to mix your own potting soil, use the following recipe.

To make about 1 cubic yard of soil, take:

- 14 cubic feet of peat moss or composted fir or pine bark
- 14 cubic feet of perlite

Dump the ingredients in a pile and roughly mix them. Dampen the mix as you go. Dry peat moss is far easier to wet with warm water than with cool water.

Spread these fertilizers over the rough mix:

- 5 pounds of ground limestone
- 5 pounds of fertilizer containing magnesium, sulfur, manganese, iron, and zinc.

Mix by shoveling (use a scoop shovel) the ingredients into a cone-shape pile, letting each shovelful slide down the cone. To get a thoroughly mixed product, repeat the cone building three to five times.

If you are not going to use the mix right away, store it in plastic bags or plastic garbage cans. To mix smaller quantities reduce the amounts of the ingredients proportionately. The nutrients in the mix will last about three to four weeks. Then begin fertilizing according to the instructions on page 34.

SELECTING A CONTAINER

When choosing a container consider its size, durability, and weight. A small plant such as a calamondin orange can be grown for years in a gallon-size pot. Many others should be moved to increasingly larger containers until they're in 15-gallon pots. Containers larger than 15 gallons are unwieldy and difficult to move.

Large clay, stone, and ceramic containers are durable but can be heavy. Wood containers are attractive and generally lightweight; unless treated with a nontoxic preservative, however, the constant contact with wet soil causes them to rot quickly. Plastic containers are light and durable and available in many designs. Pots made of modern composite materials or polystyrene are lightweight, long-lasting, and fabricated to resemble many kinds of materials. Whichever container you choose, make certain it has drainage holes.

▲ Bright light and high humidity are ideal conditions for growing citrus indoors in containers. 'Fairchild' mandarin (left) and 'Eureka' lemon (right) are growing well in this sunny room.

◀ A warm greenhouse is ideal to grow containerized bananas and other subtropical plants through winter in cold climates.

CARING FOR PLANTS IN CONTAINERS

▶ Rootbound container-grown trees are difficult to water and fertilize. To remedy the problem remove the plant from its pot and lightly prune the roots. Repot in the same container or slightly larger one.

▲ Hand pollinating citrus flowers may help fruit set on trees grown indoors.

Fertilizing

Frequent watering leaches nutrients rapidly. To compensate feed plants at least once a month with a liquid fertilizer according to the label instructions. Many gardeners prefer to feed as often as weekly, especially in hot-summer areas, where watering is a constant chore. Begin feeding in early spring and stop in late summer or early fall to avoid encouraging late, frost-sensitive growth. Fast-growing plants such as banana may need more frequent feeding. Micronutrients can also leach quickly from container soils, so use a complete fertilizer containing micronutrients. Such fertilizers can also be used for foliar applications.

Granular fertilizers can also be used on container plants, but they need time to dissolve. Nutrients are not immediately available to the roots. Slow-release fertilizer provides nutrients over time, from weeks to months depending on the product. It can be useful in maintaining a steady supply of nutrients, but you may need to supplement with liquid fertilizer during peak growth.

Root pruning

Sooner or later your plants—even those well adapted to containers—will begin to run out of root space. When this happens, the dense root ball becomes harder to water, the plant grows slowly, and fruit production declines. A solution, although it may seem a drastic one, is to prune the roots. First prune the top of the plant, reducing its size by at least one-third to compensate for the roots you are about to prune off. Next remove the plant from the container and cut off one-fourth to one-third (no more than 2 to 3 inches depending on the size of the pot) of the outside of the root ball with a sharp knife. Then place the plant back in the pot with fresh soil and water thoroughly. Done properly, root pruning quickly invigorates a rootbound plant.

Removing a large plant from a big container can be difficult, and you'll probably need help doing it. A better idea is to plan ahead and build a container with sides that are easily removed. With a little creative carpentry you can construct functional and attractive containers with slip-away sides or removal bolts.

WATERING PLANTS IN CONTAINERS

Plants grown in containers require more frequent watering than those grown in the ground. Dark pots dry out faster than light-colored ones, and porous pots made of wood or clay dry out faster than those of nonporous plastic, glazed ceramic, or polystyrene.

Apply enough water so the entire root ball becomes wet. This may take several passes with the hose. Make sure the water is not just running down the space between the root ball and container, a common occurrence if the plant has gone too long without water.

A drip irrigation system connected to an automatic timer is a great way to simplify container watering, especially in hot climates. Look for emitters and connections specifically designed for pots. Most nurseries and garden centers carry a good selection.

In areas with salty water, such as the Southwest, be sure to leach the soil well by adding enough water so that 10 to 20 percent of the water applied drains from the bottom of the container.

You can get a good idea of whether a plant needs water by gently tipping the container. If it feels light, the plant needs water; if it feels heavy, the plant can probably go a while longer.

GROWING SUBTROPICAL FRUITS IN COLD CLIMATES

Tender fruiting plants such as banana, papaya, and fig have been grown in cold climates for centuries. Orangeries, large greenhouses for overwintering potted citrus, date to 16th-century Europe. Some small-fruited types of citrus—for example calamondin orange and 'Otaheite' orange—have long been popular houseplants.

Subtropical fruits are becoming more popular in colder climates. However, many of the common rules change when you move subtropical fruits indoors, whether to a greenhouse, cool basement, or sunny windowsill. Many of these plants need pampering and more effort than the average houseplant.

The rewards are worth it, however. Colorful foliage, fragrant blossoms, and tasty fruits year-round are possible with proper care and variety selection. You'll have to follow a few rules for growing subtropical fruit in cold climates, especially if you expect to enjoy fresh fruit. The various plants require different conditions. Some are best grown in a warm greenhouse all year. Others should be grown outdoors in summer, then moved to a cool but frost-free location in winter. Despite these variations, a few guidelines apply to all potted tropicals.

Make smooth transitions

Take your time moving plants from one location to another. If you're putting plants outside after a long winter indoors, do it gradually. Place them in a shady spot first. Slowly expose the plants to increasing amounts of sun over several weeks to help prevent sunburned foliage. Also be alert for late-spring frosts.

Move plants from outdoors to indoors at an equally slow pace. Give them less and less sun until they're ready to come inside. Before bringing a plant indoors, hose it down to wash off dust or dirt on the leaves. If necessary, spray to control pests, which will multiply when brought indoors.

Maintain high humidity

The dry heat that circulates through most homes during the cold months severely shocks plants that have been outside all summer and may cause them to lose their leaves. Do everything possible to increase the humidity around the plants: Place the containers on a tray of rocks partially submerged in water, group the plants so they can humidify each other, or buy a humidifier. Also keep plants away from heat vents.

Adjust care to conditions

Once the plants are indoors, they won't need as much water, but don't allow them to dry out completely. They won't need much light either if you are trying to keep plants cool and dormant until spring. But if you are trying to ripen fruit, the more light the better. Consider supplemental illumination with artificial lights. Adjust the feeding according to how you want the plant to grow, but in general feed lightly if at all.

A sunny atrium is a perfect spot to overwinter tender container-grown fruit trees, such as citrus and banana, in cold regions.

BEST SUBTROPICAL FRUITS FOR CONTAINERS

Almost any plant can be grown in a container if the pot is large enough. Some plants, however, adapt better than others to container growing. Most of these plants suited to containers are small, so moving them to ever larger pots can be done at a leisurely pace, and they won't get so large that they become difficult to move.

Banana Conditions must be exact to ripen fruit—as hot and sunny as possible with high humidity. The only sure way to produce these conditions is to put the plant in a greenhouse. You also need to be attentive to soil moisture levels. In a warm spot a fast-growing plant like banana needs lots of water. Conversely, if the conditions are cool be careful not to overwater.

Choose dwarf banana varieties. If everything goes according to plan, they can bear fruit within 18 months of planting.

Dragonfruit Ideally suited for pots or hanging baskets dragonfruit can be moved indoors to a well lit location over winter. It makes a stunning indoor plant with colorful flowers and fruits. Hand pollinate the blooms and avoid overwatering.

Dwarf citrus More types of citrus are grown in cold climates than any other subtropical fruit. Acid citrus types such as 'Meyer' lemon, calamondin orange, kumquat, and lime are the most popular simply because they tend to be

► **An orange tree right outside your entry door makes a welcoming statement to guests and is convenient for harvesting fresh fruit for breakfast.**

◄ **Lime trees are beautiful and productive when grown in large pots. They make a great ornamental accent in the landscape.**

everblooming, don't need heat to sweeten, and ripen in a relatively short time. If you have a greenhouse, however, you can grow almost any variety of citrus.

You can treat citrus a number of different ways. If you keep the trees in a cool location, below 55°F, they will remain dormant but the fruit will still ripen. This is usually the least stressful way of overwintering the trees. Kept warmer many will continue to grow and bloom during winter, but they'll need bright light and high humidity for healthy growth. In this case a greenhouse is ideal.

Any citrus grown indoors has a greater chance of setting fruit if hand pollinated. Use a small artist's brush to spread pollen from one flower to another.

Feijoa Also known as pineapple guava, feijoa is one of the most rugged subtropical plants. Kept cool (45° to 55°F) in winter it will remain dormant and then flower when taken outdoors the following spring. The fruits ripen in midsummer, usually about four months after the flowers open. Feijoa can also be grown in a greenhouse.

Fig The easiest subtropical fruit to grow in cold climates, fig is deciduous and relatively hardy. In many areas it can be overwintered if covered with a thick mulch or protected as illustrated on page 82. It produces two crops a year and often bears fruit the first year after planting. A fig grown in a container can simply be moved to a garage, greenhouse, or basement and taken back outside when the weather warms in spring.

Guava Both tropical and strawberry guava can be overwintered indoors, but strawberry guava is more adaptable and more easily withstands the rigors of dramatically changing conditions. It is also more likely to be everblooming, and the fruits ripen over a shorter period. Tropical guava is best adapted to hot, humid greenhouse conditions. Treat guava as you would citrus, but prune regularly to keep the plant compact.

Loquat One of the easier plants to bring to fruit indoors, loquat grows well under a variety of indoor conditions and is sometimes sold as a houseplant. The plant blooms in fall, and if it is kept cool after the fruits set, a crop should ripen the following spring. For best results grow loquat outdoors in summer and prune in spring to keep the plant compact.

Papaya Best kept in a greenhouse, papaya is unlikely to survive without year-round high heat and humidity. If you can provide these conditions, your chances of enjoying fruit are good. Just remember to grow at least three plants to ensure the presence of male and female flowers for pollination (see page 103 for more details). Low-growing varieties of Hawaiian papaya, such as 'Solo', are best for indoor culture.

Passionfruit The passionfruit vine is a handsome addition to a greenhouse or patio in summer. Flowering is triggered by day length and is more profuse when the

▲ **Assorted citrus trees and annual flowers growing in large clay pots add style, color, and fragrance to a small patio.**

plant's roots are cramped in a pot. Fruit set is most likely under humid conditions; the fruits ripen three to four months after flowering. Prune to keep the plant within bounds. Although the vine will grow as a houseplant, it will seldom flower or set fruit in low-light interior conditions.

Tree tomato The tree tomato and its relatives in the Solanaceae family, such as pepino, are good indoor/outdoor plants for cold climates. They grow quickly from seed, fruit at a young age, and adapt well to a variety of indoor conditions.

HOW TO MOVE LARGE CONTAINER PLANTS

Avoid injury and hard work by preplanning how you will move heavy, container-grown fruit trees. Nurseries offer many types of wheeled platforms or watering trays.

PVC pipe or wooden dowels and a wide board simplify moving heavy pots. Place the pot on the board and roll the pipes forward. Move the rear pipe to the front when it is no longer covered by the board.

A dolly is a great tool for easily moving large containers. It works best on level ground. You may need to fashion a ramp of boards to go over door thresholds.

CITRUS

▼ Beautiful and bountiful citrus trees provide fresh fruit from fall through spring and even into the summer months.

HISTORY OF CITRUS

◀ Citrus trees can be grown in the Southeast along the Gulf Coast and in the Southwest in the deserts of Arizona and California as well as coastal regions of the West. The map at left indicates the primary growing regions in red. With a protected microclimate and more cold-hardy varieties, citrus can also be grown in the regions in yellow.

Tracing the migration and development of citrus fruit is like taking a course in world history. Citrus varieties were used as medicinals in ancient India and in the Persian Empire; they were pampered in the orangeries of Louis XIV at Versailles and, centuries after being introduced to the New World by Christopher Columbus, savored by Americans as an important fruit crop.

No fruit can boast a more glorious past. Citrus fruits have served humans as tributes to rulers, symbols of religious devotion, expressions of love, additions to beautiful landscapes, and important foods to preserve health.

Citrus plants are some of the most rewarding for home gardeners to grow. Consider the qualities of citrus: lustrous, emerald green or variegated foliage, sweetly perfumed white blossoms, and brightly colored fruits that hang like jewels from the branches. Even types of citrus that are usually considered inedible, such as sour orange, are used as ornamentals.

Citrus fruits also offer great variety. Mature plants range in size from small shrubs, such as 'Improved Meyer' lemon, to large trees, such as vigorously growing grapefruit. Leaves range from the small, pointed foliage of 'Chinotto' sour orange to the large, lush, tropical-looking leaves of pummelo.

The fruit can be as small as a bean on kumquat or almost as large as a volleyball on pummelo.

Fruit color may be the yellow of lemons, citrons, and pummelos; the bright orange of sweet orange varieties; or the brilliant red-orange of such fruit as 'Temple' tangor, 'Dancy' mandarin, and 'Minneola' tangelo. Fruits may also have a distinctive red blush as in 'Moro' or 'Sanguinelli' blood oranges or striped as in 'Variegated Calamondin' orange or 'Variegated Pink Eureka' lemon.

The colors of the flesh and juice of citrus fruits are as variable as the colors of the rind. Lemons and limes have pale yellowish green flesh and juice. The most brilliantly colored juice comes from 'Moro' blood orange and 'Star Ruby' grapefruit.

The myriad flavors of citrus fruits are unmatched by any other type of fruit. You can choose among the highly acidic and aromatic flavors of lemons and limes; the tangy spiciness of mandarins; the sprightly sweetness of oranges; the sweet, rich, almost syrupy taste of 'Kinnow' mandarin; and the aromatic flavor and perfumed bouquet of 'Chandler' pummelo. Even the bitter flavor of sour oranges is esteemed by connoisseurs of marmalades and bitters.

Before Western civilization discovered the edible sweet orange, citrus trees were grown in orangeries for the fragrance of the flowers and peel. Louis XIV grew citrus not for the fruit but so his stately banquets could be blessed with the fragrance of the blossoms. The rind of 'Bergamot' sour orange is still used to make eau de cologne, the most widely used of toilet waters, and it is an important ingredient in many other perfume products.

ADAPTATION

▲ Citrus fruit from large to small: 'Chandler' pummelo, 'Star Ruby' grapefruit, 'Minneola' tangelo, 'Robertson' navel orange, 'Valencia' orange, 'Moro' blood orange, 'Dancy' mandarin, 'Eureka' lemon, 'Bearss' lime, 'Chinotto' sour orange, 'Rangpur' lime, 'Nagami' kumquat, 'Golden Bean' kumquat.

It's hard to imagine a fruit more drastically affected by climate variations than citrus.

Seasonal temperature differences have the most important influence on adaptation. The lowest temperature at which growth takes place is 55°F; the highest is approximately 100°F. Some differences exist among varieties and species. The optimum temperature for growth of oranges ranges between 70° and 90°F.

Hardiness differs according to species and sometimes variety of citrus. Trees can usually withstand temperatures 3 to 4 degrees lower than those that will damage the fruit. Also ripe fruit can withstand lower temperatures than can immature or green fruit. For this reason gardeners in marginal citrus areas select early-maturing varieties, which usually ripen before the first frost. Fully dormant 'Satsuma' mandarin trees can withstand temperatures as low as 18°F without defoliation. Kumquats may tolerate temperatures a degree or two colder. Most other mandarins can take 22° to 23°F; grapefruit and oranges 23° to 24°F; lemons 26° to 27°F; and limes 28°F. The average freezing point for mature fruits of 'Satsuma' mandarins and 'Temple' tangors is 28°F. Ripe navel oranges freeze at 27° to 28°F. Half-ripe navel orange fruits are damaged at 28° to 29°F.

Duration of cold is also important in determining whether fruit will be damaged. It usually takes three or four hours at 27° to 28°F to injure navel oranges, but it may take only 30 to 60 minutes at 29°F to injure small lemons.

Citrus fruits also have heat requirements. All varieties of grapefruit require a long, hot growing season to reach peak quality and sweetness. They are best adapted to Texas, Florida, and low-elevation desert areas of Arizona and California. Other types of citrus have lower heat requirements and can be grown in cooler areas. Lemons have the lowest heat requirement and can be grown in the cool coastal areas of California.

The many citrus varieties can be grown outdoors year-round in one or more of the following regions. To learn where each variety is best adapted, see pages 46 to 61.

■ **California (CA)** This large area includes both the northern and the southern parts of the state. Summers are usually hot and dry; most rain falls in the winter. Southern California, with its many frost-free microclimates, is a traditional citrus area and offers many opportunities from the coast to inland areas. Northern California also has frost-free areas, but along the coast the summers are too cool for many varieties. Many more types of citrus are adapted to the inland areas of Northern California, where there is more summer heat but also a greater chance of cold winter weather.

■ **California and Arizona deserts (DS)** These low-elevation areas have extremely hot summers, warm winters, strong sunlight, and gusty winds. Varieties with high heat requirements are best here, but sunburn and wind damage are very common.

■ **Florida (FL)** This hot, humid region has many frost-free areas, although occasionally a freeze devastates citrus throughout the state. Rainfall is spread throughout the year. Hardy and early-ripening varieties are the best choices for Northern Florida.

■ **Texas and the Gulf Coast (GC)** These areas are usually hot and humid with some rainfall the year round. West Texas is drier and warmer; some areas resemble desert climates. Mild-winter South Texas is home to a commercial citrus industry, but even some more northern areas, including southern Louisiana where 'Satsuma' mandarins are grown, have a history of commercial citrus. Cold waves of arctic air are common in winter, so hardy, early varieties that ripen before winter are best.

Devastating diseases such as citrus greening and citrus canker, spread by strong hurricanes, have had a dramatic impact on growing citrus in Florida. Quarantines have restricted movement of nursery trees, affecting availability, and in some areas planting fruit other than citrus may be advisable. Contact your local extension service for the latest recommendations.

CLIMATE EFFECTS

Climate has a strong influence on fruit size, shape, flavor, and juice content, as well as rind color, flesh color, texture, and thickness. Climate also affects the tree's growth rate, habit, and flowering. In general, climate influences citrus in the following ways.

■ **Bloom** Trees flower earliest in hot, humid areas and latest in cool, semiarid coastal areas. Thus 'Valencia' orange reaches peak bloom in mid-March in Orlando, and in Weslaco, Texas; early April in the hot desert areas of Arizona and California; and early May in the cool coastal valleys of Central and Southern California.

■ **Maturity** Fruit grown in a hot area ripens before fruit of the same variety in a cooler area. There is a close (but not absolute) relationship between the accumulated heat units (the heat accumulation) in a growing season and date of maturity. A heat unit index is calculated by adding together all the mean daily temperatures greater than 55°F between bloom and maturity. 'Valencia' orange ripens in March in the hot, humid climates of Florida and Texas and in the hot, arid California and Arizona deserts. In cool coastal areas of California, 'Valencia' may not ripen until June.

■ **Fruit size** Fruit is usually largest in hot, humid climates, becoming progressively smaller in hot, arid climates and cool, arid ones. Varieties that produce large fruit in arid subtropical areas of California sometimes produce fruit that is too large when grown in Florida. Likewise varieties such as 'Hamlin' and 'Pineapple' oranges, which reach marketable size in Florida, are too small for commercial acceptance when grown in California.

■ **Fruit shape** Fruit tends to be longer in relation to width in hotter areas and flatter in cooler climates.

■ **Peel characteristics** Peels are thin and smooth in hot, humid Florida and Texas. In arid regions of the West, they are thicker with a rougher texture.

■ **Color development** In truly tropical areas citrus fruits are green when ripe. In hot, humid areas of Florida and Texas, rind color remains pale in most varieties. The most intense color develops in arid climates of the West, where low temperatures prevail for several weeks before harvest.

The red color in the flesh and rind of blood oranges is due to the presence of the pigment anthocyanin. This pigment develops best in warm, intermediate climates, such as those in the interior valleys of Central and Southern California.

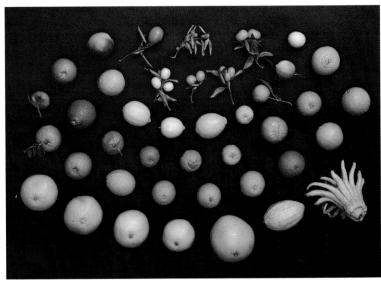

Red coloration is less intense in the hot desert areas of California and Arizona. In humid climates blood oranges rarely develop good red color.

A different pigment, called lycopene, produces red in grapefruits and pummelos. In this case a strong color is directly related to high temperatures during maturation. Thus red varieties of grapefruit and pummelos develop their most intense color in hot climates. Grapefruits and pummelos develop little or no red in cool climates.

■ **Juice content** Citrus fruits are juiciest when they're grown in hot, humid climates and less juicy in regions that are hot and arid or cool and humid.

■ **Flavor** Sugar and acid are the main components of citrus flavor that are influenced by climate. Fruits grown in arid climates that have a cold period before the fruit matures contain more acid and a better balance between sugars and acids than those grown in humid climates. This usually means that fruit from arid areas has a richer flavor, although many people prefer the sweeter taste of fruit grown in humid areas. Overall the percentage of acid in the juice is higher in fruit grown in cooler climates.

■ **Tree habit** Trees grow fastest in hot, humid climates and slowest in cooler areas. For that reason trees in colder climates are usually more compact.

When all these effects are combined, the result is that the fruit of a variety grown in the Southeast is lighter in color, has a thinner rind, is juicier, and tastes sweeter than the same variety grown in the West. This is the main reason the more colorful, richer-flavored, commercially grown California oranges are usually sold fresh, and Florida oranges are made into juice.

PROPAGATION

▲ **Fragrant citrus flowers bloom mostly in spring.**

▲ **Fruits develop from late spring through fall and winter.**

▲ **Depending on variety, fruit is ready to harvest from fall through spring.**

Most citrus trees are propagated by budding the desired variety onto a specific type of rootstock. Budded trees are preferred over seedling trees because they are reliably true to type, come into production sooner, and benefit from qualities for which the rootstock was chosen, such as disease resistance, greater cold tolerance, dwarfing, better fruit quality, earlier maturity, and adaptation to adverse soil conditions.

■ **Rootstocks** 'Troyer' and 'Carrizo' citranges and 'Swingle' citrumelo are the most widely used rootstocks for standard citrus trees, but there are many others, each with specific adaptation or resistance to particular pests. Unfortunately, few nurseries label rootstocks, so unless you propagate your own or ask the wholesale grower, you may never be sure which rootstock a tree is grown on. Cooperative extension service and nursery websites have the most complete information on specific rootstocks if you want to propagate your own trees.

Trifoliate orange (*Poncirus trifoliata*) is the most common dwarfing rootstock. It is also disease resistant and causes fruit to ripen slightly earlier. Because it is also more cold tolerant than other rootstocks, it is highly recommended in cold climates. Trifoliate orange dwarfs most varieties by 30 to 50 percent in home gardens. The trifoliate variety 'Flying Dragon' provides even more dwarfing; trees on this rootstock will not grow much taller than 5 to 6 feet high.

Some citrus, including limes and 'Improved Meyer' lemon, are often grown on their own roots. Although these cutting-grown trees lack the attributes provided by many rootstocks, they will resprout true to type from the roots if the top is frozen to the ground.

■ **Seedlings** Citrus seeds often produce two or more seedlings as a result of a phenomenon known as nucellar embryony. One of these seedlings is the result of pollination and will produce a tree that has traits from both parents. The others, which are not the result of pollination, are nucellar seedlings, which are identical to the tree from which they came. Different varieties of citrus produce nucellar seedlings at different rates. Varieties that produce a large percentage of nucellar seedlings can be grown from seed because a large percentage of the seedling trees will be identical to the parent. Nucellar seedlings are often used as citrus rootstocks.

Fresh citrus seeds germinate easily at soil temperatures between 80° and 90°F. They lose their viability rapidly when allowed to dry out. To store citrus seeds properly, pack them in moist (but not wet) peat moss or vermiculite and keep them in the refrigerator for up to six months.

POLLINATION

Most varieties are self-fruitful, but some varieties produce more fruit when pollinated by another variety. This need for cross-pollination is noted in the "Comments" section of the variety charts. Pollination can also influence seediness in some varieties. Certain mandarins, for example, will be seedy if a suitable pollinator variety is nearby. If no pollinator is close, they will have few or no seeds. The seeded fruit tends to be larger.

LANDSCAPING WITH CITRUS

◄ 'Moro' blood orange dominates this entry garden. As visitors climb the stairs between the entry pillars and follow the walkway behind the tree to the front door, they can appreciate the tree's evergreen foliage, colorful fruits, and attractive blooms.

With handsome dark green foliage, fragrant flowers, and colorful fruit, most citrus varieties make exceptional landscape plants. They can be used as individual specimens, evergreen shade trees, and screens or even pruned as hedges or espaliers. Although heavy pruning reduces yields, many types of citrus, particularly lemons, can be successfully grown this way. Smaller types of citrus, including 'Improved Meyer' lemon, kumquat, 'Satsuma' mandarin, and any variety grown on 'Flying Dragon' dwarfing rootstock are ideal container plants.

When choosing specific citrus types for landscape purposes, consider the mature size of the tree, texture of the foliage, and visibility of the fruit. The large leaves of a grapefruit tree setting off beautiful clusters of yellow fruit is a wonderful combination, as is the bright orange-red orbs of 'Clementine' mandarin highlighted by fine-textured foliage. Multihued varieties, such as 'Variegated Pink Eureka' and 'Variegated Calamondin', also make distinctive landscape subjects.

Care for citrus plants grown as landscape trees with more diligence. Prune to expose the inner branching structure or to increase foliage density for screening. Fertilize consistently to maintain a deep green color, and watch carefully for pest problems such as scale insects.

▲ Fragrant flowers and flavorful fruits make citrus one of the best of the ornamental edibles. This landscape has kaffir lime conveniently located right off the deck.

SITE SELECTION AND PLANTING

Citrus trees are usually sold in containers but are sometimes available balled and burlapped. Trees purchased by mail may be shipped bare root. The best time to plant is in early spring, after the danger of frost has passed. For best results the soil pH should be between 6 and 7.

All citrus trees prefer maximum exposure to sunlight, but in desert climates some light shade during the hottest part of the day may prevent sunburned fruit. In cool climates plant in the warmest possible microclimate, such as against a light-colored, south-facing wall. Avoid low spots where cold air can accumulate.

CARING FOR CITRUS

Most citrus trees are easy to care for, requiring minimal pruning and infrequent pest control. All they usually need is regular watering and fertilizing.

Watering

Adequate soil moisture is essential for healthy growth and good fruit production. Drought during bloom causes the flowers to drop and results in poor fruit set. Lack of moisture during the growing season causes fruit drop and low yield. Prolonged drought will defoliate and eventually kill the tree. At the other extreme standing water and poorly drained soils are almost always lethal to citrus trees. Plant your tree in well-drained soil and water it regularly during dry periods.

Fertilizing

Citrus trees must be fertilized regularly. The number of applications depends on the region; consult the chart at right for timing and rates.

Soils in some areas are also deficient in micronutrients. In these cases the trees need foliar micronutrient sprays.

Pruning

A citrus tree generally does not require regular pruning to be productive and is usually allowed to develop on its own. You may, however, want to prune to control the size of lemon trees and other vigorous types of citrus. Prune to remove overcrowded branches and thin the interior growth to keep trees bearing throughout the canopy and to reduce pest buildups. Avoid excessive pruning, which can expose bark to sunburn. Most citrus can be sheared as hedges or trained as espaliers and still produce some fruit.

Rejuvenate old overgrown trees by severe pruning. Known as skeletonizing, this radical pruning method involves removing all limbs greater than 1 to 2 inches in diameter. If you are going to skeletonize a tree, do so in early spring so it can regrow during the next growing season. The tree won't produce any fruit for about two years, but when it does begin to bear again, the fruit usually will be larger than normal. Skeletonizing is effective only on otherwise healthy trees and is not a cure for diseases.

The bark of citrus trees is susceptible to sunburn, especially after severe pruning. After heavy pruning always paint exposed branches and trunks with water-base white paint (diluted with an equal amount of water) or commercially available whitewash. Also protect the bark of newly planted trees by using tree wrap, plastic tree guards, available from nurseries, or by painting diluted water-base white paint on the trunk.

Controlling pests and diseases

Vigorously growing trees usually have few problems, but even robust trees occasionally become infested with aphids, leafminers, mites, psyllids, scale insects, snails, thrips, or whiteflies. Trees growing in poorly drained soils often succumb to diseases such as phytophthora root rot.

FERTILIZING YOUNG CITRUS TREES

Although in some areas nitrogen may be all that is needed, most home garden trees will benefit from a complete fertilizer including zinc, iron, and manganese.

California, Arizona, and Texas		
Years after planting	Number of applications per year (Feb–Sept)	Pounds of actual nitrogen per application*
1	3	0.1
2	3	0.2
3	2	0.4
4	2	0.45
5	2	0.5
6	2	0.55
7	2	0.6
8–10 (mature)	2	0.6–0.75

Florida and the Gulf Coast		
1	4–5	0.1
2	4	0.2
3	3	0.3
4	3	0.4
5	3	0.45
6	3	0.45–0.5
7–10 (mature)	3	0.5

*See page 22 for an example calculation of the pounds of actual nitrogen in a fertilizer.

HARVEST AND STORAGE

Citrus fruits mature at various times of the year. Early varieties of oranges and mandarins ripen in October or November of the year in which they bloom. Late varieties of orange, mandarin, and grapefruit mature from February to May the following year. In hot, humid regions, such as Florida and Texas, the fruits mature slightly before the same varieties grown in the hot, dry deserts of California and Arizona and well before fruit in the cool coastal areas of California.

In California 'Washington' navel and 'Valencia' oranges are grown in three distinct climates—cool, intermediate, and hot. As a result California growers harvest fresh oranges throughout the year. Navel oranges mature in November in the warmest areas, but they may be picked as late as June of the following year in cooler areas. 'Valencia' begins to mature in February in the desert; in cooler climates the harvest extends into October.

The only sure way to determine maturity is to taste the fruit. Color is a poor indicator of ripeness because many fruits develop fully colored rinds months before they can be eaten. Lemons, limes, and other acid citrus fruits are an exception. They can be picked whenever they reach acceptable size and juice content.

Once mature most citrus fruits can be stored on the tree for several weeks and picked as needed. Mandarins are an exception, holding their fruit for shorter periods than oranges, grapefruits, or lemons. When mandarins have been on the tree too long, they lose their juice and the pulp dries out. A puffy rind is an indication that the fruit is overly mature.

Most citrus fruits can be stored in the refrigerator for at least two to three weeks. Under dry conditions at room temperature, fruits develop off flavors, wither, and lose their looks within a week to 10 days.

▲ These 'Cara Cara' navel oranges have a deep orange rind and have developed their characteristic pink flesh color. Their sweet taste indicates that they are ready to harvest.

Types of Citrus

Citron

The fruit of citron (*Citrus medica*) is large and thick-skinned and resembles a lemon. The tree is scraggly and frost sensitive, but it is sometimes grown as a novelty or for the ceremonies associated with the Jewish Feast of Tabernacles. 'Etrog' is the most commonly planted variety, but the fingered citron 'Buddha's Hand' has a more unusual fruit shape and is often used in floral displays.

■ **Using citrons** Although a citron may look like a lemon, its pulpy flesh yields little or no juice. Thus only the thick rind of the citron is used—candied, for flavoring, and in marmalade. Many people have seen only the candied and dyed citron rind, sold for use in fruitcakes and Christmas puddings.

'Buddha's Hand' citron is an ornamental. In a pinch its "fingers" may be grated and used for flavoring, but the tentacles of this unusual fruit are mostly pith (the zest is almost impossible to separate), and many other fruits are much better for preserves.

'Etrog' citron is used in Jewish religious ceremonies, and its zest is used in cooking.

The fantastically bizarre 'Buddha's Hand' fingered citron is aptly named.

Grapefruit

'Oroblanco' grapefruit hybrid is sweeter than regular grapefruit varieties.

'Flame' grapefruit

'Melogold' grapefruit hybrid

'Star Ruby' grapefruit

Grapefruit appears to have originated in the West Indies. Researchers believe it is a naturally occurring hybrid of pummelo and sweet orange.

The fruit is borne on a large tree with big deep green leaves; it requires a long, hot growing season to reach peak quality. However, its ability to hang on the tree for long periods without deteriorating allows it to attain acceptable flavor in cooler regions.

There are two types of fruit: white fleshed and pigmented. 'Duncan' and 'Marsh Seedless' have white flesh, while 'Flame', 'Ruby', 'Redblush', 'Rio Red', and 'Star Ruby' develop pink to red flesh and a reddish rind in hot climates. Pigmented types tend not to color well in cool climates, but newer introductions such as 'Flame' are more likely to do so.

'Oroblanco', 'Melogold', and 'Cocktail' are grapefruit-pummelo hybrids developed by the University of California. They bear incredibly juicy fruit with a sweet, low-acid flavor and are good choices for cooler climates.

Using grapefruit Although grapefruit is commonplace and available nearly all year nowadays, it is still often considered an elegant treat. In salads grapefruit is as versatile as orange, though its tartness calls for a different treatment. Arrange sections of grapefruit on a plate with greens as bitter as watercress. But offset its tartness with one of the sweet vinegars (balsamic, raspberry, or a good cider vinegar) and a fruity olive or walnut oil. Consider adding vegetables such as parboiled artichoke hearts or roasted sweet red peppers or even bits of sweet fruit such as dried dates to a grapefruit salad. Avocados and grapefruit are a classic combination.

'Rio Red' grapefruit grows best in hot summer climates.

Grapefruit *(continued)*

There is basically no flavor difference between pink and white grapefruit, but there is a difference between seedy and seedless fruit. Seedy fruits have a richer, more pronounced flavor and separate into segments easily. For this reason they are often grown for commercial processing. If you want the most intensely flavored juice, consider growing 'Duncan', a seedy variety.

Cooked and sweetened with sugar, grapefruit makes excellent marmalade and candied peel. Take advantage of a prolific harvest by making freshly squeezed, chilled grapefruit juice and serving it at brunch. Or make a fancy grapefruit sorbet and serve it as a palate cleanser or with delicate wafers as a light dessert.

If purchasing fresh grapefruits, choose ones that are heavy (indicating a high percentage of juice) and thin skinned. Ignore superficial scars and russeting; they have no effect on quality.

'Cocktail' grapefruit hybrid

'Marsh' grapefruit

GRAPEFRUIT AND HYBRIDS

Variety	Adaptation	Fruit description	Comments
'Cocktail'	CA, DS	Medium, midseason, yellow to orange rind, seedy, sweet, juicy, orange flesh.	Pummelo-mandarin hybrid from the University of California.
'Duncan'	FL, GC	Large, somewhat early, seedy, very juicy, white flesh. Excellent flavor. Holds well on tree.	Large, vigorous, productive tree. Attractive habit, dark green foliage. Reputed to be most cold-tolerant grapefruit.
'Flame'	CA, DS, FL, GC	Large, midseason to late, rind often blushed pink, seedless, deep pink flesh.	Large tree with showy clusters of fruit.
'Marsh'	CA, DS, FL, GC	Medium, late maturing, seedless, white flesh, very juicy. Holds extremely well on tree, stores well.	Large, vigorous, spreading tree requires high summer heat. Attractive clusters of fruit, glossy leaves.
'Melogold'	CA, DS	Large, early, thick rind, seedless, white flesh, rich, sweet. Often borne in clusters.	Large tree. Pummelo-grapefruit hybrid. Best in interior California but needs less heat than grapefruit. Does well in cooler areas.
'Oroblanco'	CA, DS	Medium to large, early, thick rind, seedless, extremely juicy, white flesh, distinctive sweet flavor. Does not hold well on tree.	Large tree. Pummelo-grapefruit hybrid. Best in interior California but needs less heat than grapefruit.
'Redblush' ('Ruby', 'Red Marsh')	CA, DS, FL, GC	Medium, midseason, similar to 'Marsh' except flesh and rind have crimson tinge. Holds very well on tree.	Large, vigorous tree identical to 'Marsh'. Needs heat to develop red color.
'Star Ruby'	CA, DS, FL, GC	Medium, midseason, seedless, juicy, deep red flesh. Holds well on tree.	Medium-size, open tree. Developed for Texas; needs heat. 'Rio Red' is similar but bears more consistently.

Kumquat and its hybrids

Hardy species of *Fortunella*, kumquats are attractive trees densely covered with small leaves. They can get quite large on vigorous rootstocks but are usually small and compact, ideal for containers. Unlike most other citrus they bloom in the heat of summer.

Because they are hardy to at least 18°F, kumquats have been used for hybridization with other citrus, such as limes (limequats) and oranges (orangequats), both of which are ornamental. 'Nagami' and 'Meiwa' are the most widely available varieties of kumquat, but some types with larger fruit can sometimes be found. They include sweet-tart 'Marumi' and the sweet, juicy, bell-shape 'Fukushu'.

▌ **Using kumquats** The fruits are usually preserved and used whole as garnishes for meats or made into marmalade. They are also delightful when eaten fresh: Just roll and squeeze a fruit between your fingers to combine the sweet flavor of the skin with the tart flavor of the pulp. Hybrids of kumquat range in sweetness. Orangequat is the sweetest (sweeter than kumquat) and

'Marumi' kumquat

'Nagami' kumquat

'Nordmann' seedless kumquat

limequat is very tart. Limequats can be substituted for limes in prepared foods.

Kumquats are found in grocery stores from November through spring. Their size and seediness depend on maturity at harvest time and on the variety, but all are edible out of hand.

In addition to their culinary value, kumquats are also decorative and are often used in holiday season centerpieces. Their bright orange skins contrast nicely with a few bright green leaves left on their stems. Kumquat hybrids also make attractive table decorations. Orangequat is a little larger than kumquat and bright orange; the limequat is smaller and bright yellow.

KUMQUAT HYBRIDS

Variegated calamondin

'Indio' mandarinquat

'Eustis' limequat

'Nippon' orangequat

KUMQUAT AND HYBRIDS

Variety	Adaptation	Fruit description	Comments
Kumquat 'Nagami'	CA, DS, FL, GC	Small, oval, early, rind slightly sweet, flesh acidic, little juice, used primarily for canning. Holds very well on tree.	Small to medium, vigorous tree with small, dark leaves, fine branches. Excellent container plant. Cold tolerant. 'Nordmann' is a seedless type.
Kumquat 'Meiwa'	CA, DS, FL, GC	Small, round, late fruit, sweet rind and flesh, good for fresh eating. Holds very well on tree.	Small to medium tree with smaller leaves and more open habit than 'Nagami'. Very cold tolerant.
Limequat 'Eustis'	CA, DS, FL, GC	Medium, tart, juicy, light yellow when mature, resembles lime when immature.	Hybrid of Mexican lime and kumquat; tree resembles lime but is much more cold tolerant. Attractive, small, nearly thornless, suitable for containers. 'Lakeland' is similar.
Limequat 'Tavares'	CA, DS, FL, GC	Large (up to 3" long), oblong, yellow, excellent lime flavor. Holds well on tree.	Beautiful, compact tree. Hardy.
Mandarinquat 'Indio'	CA, DS, FL, GC	Large, bell shape, sweet orange rind, tart orange interior.	Attractive, compact tree. Mandarin-kumquat hybrid.
Orangequat 'Nippon'	CA, DS, FL, GC	Medium, sweet, juicy, rind and pulp deep orange. Larger than the kumquats.	Small, attractive, compact tree.

Lemon

'Variegated Pink Eureka' lemon has pink flesh, variegated leaves and fruit rinds.

Lemon trees are among the most vigorous of the citrus family. Standard trees can reach more than 20 feet high. They respond well to pruning, however, and are one of the few citrus trees that should be regularly cut back to keep them compact and the fruit within reach. Lemons are attractive plants with light green leaves that have a reddish tinge when young.

The plants are best adapted to the western states, where fruits remain small and trees are less likely to be infected with disease. In hot, humid climates limes are a better choice. In coastal California lemon trees usually bear several crops a year. In warmer areas harvest is fall through winter. Pick lemons whenever they reach acceptable size and color.

'Improved Meyer' lemon is not a true lemon but rather a lemon-orange hybrid. It is a popular lemon substitute, especially among dessert lovers. It has a distinctive flowery flavor, bright orange-yellow flesh, and a higher sugar content than a true lemon, although still a tart flavor. It was discovered near Beijing by Frank N. Meyer, a USDA plant explorer, and was introduced to the United States in 1908. Since then its handsome, compact habit has made it one of the most popular dooryard citrus varieties. 'Improved Meyer' lemon trees are productive for years in containers and can be trained to form a dense hedge.

■ **Using lemons** A bearing lemon tree nearby can become as

'Meyer' lemon

'Eureka' lemon

'Lisbon' lemon

'Seedless Lisbon' lemon has few, if any, seeds.

'Ponderosa' lemon

necessary to a cook as a kitchen herb garden. Lemon zest adds a sophisticated dimension to such diverse foods as stews, chocolate cake, and pizza. When using the rind of any citrus fruit, remember that the fragrant, flavorful oils are in the thin, pigmented outer portion, or zest, of the peel. The inner, pithy portion can be bitter. When your tree is producing too many lemons for you to consume or give away (or when lemons are particularly inexpensive at the supermarket) and you don't have time to make lemon marmalade, squeeze the juice and freeze it in a freezer tray. A plastic bag full of lemon juice cubes is a bag of gold to the cook. Make hot toddies with them in the evening (boiled with water, brown sugar, and a clove, with rum added); use them in chicken, game, or pork marinades; make lemonade; or use them to make mayonnaise, Hollandaise sauce, or a simple mixture of juice and melted butter for vegetables.

When you serve a Tuscan, Provençal, Spanish, or other hearty Mediterranean stew or braised meat, have a little dish of *gremolata* on the table for guests to sprinkle on their meat.

■ **To make gremolata** Mince 1 part lemon zest with 1 part garlic cloves and 2 parts parsley.

LEMON

Variety	Adaptation	Fruit description	Comments
'Eureka'	CA, DS	Medium, highly acidic, juicy, few seeds. Produces fruit all year along coast, spring and summer inland. Common commercial variety.	Medium, nearly thornless, moderately vigorous tree, open and spreading.
'Improved Meyer'	CA, DS, FL, GC	Medium, very juicy, slightly sweet and orange-yellow when mature, excellent flowery flavor. Few seeds. Holds well on tree.	Orange-lemon hybrid. Small to medium, nearly thornless, moderately vigorous tree. Spreading habit, good for hedges and containers. Hardy, productive, and nearly everblooming.
'Lisbon'	CA, DS	Medium, highly acidic, juicy, few seeds. Best picked when ripe; loses acidity if left on tree.	Large, vigorous, thorny, upright tree with dense foliage. Flowers and new growth tinged with purple. Most productive and cold hardy of true lemons.
'Ponderosa'	CA, DS, FL, GC	Grapefruit-size, juicy, and acidic with thick, fleshy rind. Seedy. Holds well on tree.	Small, roundheaded, thorny tree with large leaves; blooms all year. Hybrid of lemon and citron; sensitive to frost. Good subject for containers and hedges.
'Variegated Pink Eureka'	CA, DS	Starts green, red, and yellow striped; matures to yellow with green stripes and finally yellow. Interior light pink. Seedier than 'Eureka'.	Very ornamental with dark green leaves, variegated white. Often sold as 'Pink Lemonade', but juice isn't that dark.

Lime

'Bearss' lime

'Mary Ellen' sweet lime

'Thornless Mexican' lime

Limes can be divided into two groups: small-fruited 'Mexican', West Indian, or Key lime; and large-fruited 'Persian' or 'Tahiti' lime. 'Mexican' lime was once an important commercial variety and is often referred to as the bartender's lime. The deep green fruit is borne on a small, thorny tree that is very frost sensitive and best adapted to humid climates. However, its rich, aromatic flavor is so appealing that it is often grown elsewhere, even in areas where it needs frequent winter protection.

'Persian' lime is now more widely grown commercially, mainly in Mexico. 'Bearss' is the most common variety cultivated in California. The tree is a few degrees hardier than 'Mexican' lime and has a more compact, attractive habit. The fruit is lighter green than 'Mexican' but has a good lime flavor.

Harvest both types of limes when they reach acceptable size. Fully mature fruit turns from green to yellow.

'Rangpur' lime is actually an acid mandarin with small, juicy, bright orange fruit. Keiffer or kaffir lime, the foliage of which is used in some Asian cuisines, is actually a separate species, *Citrus hystrix*.

■ **Using limes** 'Mexican' (or Key) lime is the most aromatic of the limes and for that reason is preferred for marmalades, garnishes, and Key lime pie. "Authentic" Key lime pie is the subject of much argument: It is made a variety of ways, topped with a meringue or as a chiffon pie, with a short crust or with a crust made of crumbs. To make one simply substitute lime zest and juice for lemon zest and juice in your favorite lemon pie recipe.

The juicy 'Persian' lime is excellent for making limeade and marinades for meats. If thinly sliced it can be eaten, rind and all.

LIME

Variety	Adaptation	Fruit description	Comments
'Bearss' ('Tahiti', 'Persian')	CA, DS, FL, GC	Medium-small, acidic, very juicy. Usually picked green; yellow when mature. Does not hold well on tree.	Medium, vigorous, spreading tree with fragrant blossoms and shiny fruit all year in cool coastal areas. Few thorns, hardier and more attractive than 'Mexican'.
Keiffer (Kaffir, *C. hystrix*)	CA	Small, early, light green, very bumpy, intensely aromatic rind, seedy.	Thorny tree grown primarily for its leaves which are used in Asian cooking. Fruit can also be used but drops early.
'Mexican' (Key lime, West Indian lime)	CA, DS, FL, GC	Very small, juicy, acidic with distinctive aroma, the bartender's lime. Commercially picked when green; turns yellow and drops from tree when mature.	Medium, twiggy tree with dense canopy of small leaves, many short thorns. Thornless form is also available. Moderately vigorous. Very frost sensitive, needs long, hot summers for size.
Palestine Sweet (*C. limettiodes*, Indian sweet lime)	CA, DS	Small to medium, early, green turning to yellow, mildly sweet acidless flavor often described as insipid, few seeds.	Medium size, shrubby. Popular for juice. 'Mary Ellen' is a large-fruited selection.
'Rangpur'	CA, DS, FL, GC	Small to medium, very acidic, juicy, rind reddish-orange when mature. Holds very well on tree.	Medium, vigorous tree with spreading, drooping habit, few thorns. Very cold tolerant. Not a true lime (resembles mandarin) but often used as a lime substitute. 'Otaheite' is an acidless semidwarf form popular for containers.

Mandarin orange and its hybrids

'Dancy' mandarin

'Gold Nugget' mandarin

'Honey' mandarin

'Seedless Kishu' mandarin

'W. Murcott' mandarin

'Clementine' mandarin

'Page' mandarin

'Pixie' mandarin

'Ponkan' mandarin

'Satsuma' mandarin

'Shasta Gold' mandarin

'Tahoe Gold' mandarin

'Yosemite Gold' mandarin

Mandarin orange is one of the more diverse groups of citrus, with more new varieties now available than for any other citrus type. Many newer varieties are actually complex hybrids made up of several different types of citrus, including orange, pummelo, grapefruit, and other mandarins. Some mandarin oranges are better known as tangerines, a name that originated with the introduction from Tangiers of the brightly colored 'Dancy' variety. Since then many orange-red mandarins have been called tangerines even though the name has no botanical standing.

Mandarin fruits range from small to large, ripen early to late, and vary in color and flavor. The trees range from tall and upright to small and compact. Some have weeping habits. The foliage is hardier than that of orange but the fruit is not.

The fruits are often called kid-glove or loose-skin oranges because they are usually quite easy to peel.

If you choose varieties carefully, you can harvest mandarins from November to July or later. The flavor of mandarins ranges from sprightly to sweet to almost spicy. The fruit often won't hold on the tree as well as oranges, becoming puffy, dry, and insipid.

Some varieties of mandarin set more fruit if pollinated by another variety planted nearby. Others, such as 'W. Murcott' and 'Clementine', will be seedy when cross-pollinated but seedless if isolated from pollinators. Still other mandarins, such as 'Pixie', 'Satsuma', 'Gold Nugget', and 'Seedless Kishu', are always seedless.

Most mandarins produce the best-quality fruit when grown in hot-summer climates. However a few, such as 'Kara', 'Page', and 'Pixie', yield good-quality fruit in milder climates, such as coastal California.

Mandarin orange and its hybrids *(continued)*

Many mandarins are alternate bearing, producing heavy crops of small fruit one year and light crops of bigger fruit the next. Heavy pruning before bloom or fruit thinning after fruit drop during heavy set years minimizes this effect.

▋ **Tangelo** Because this is such a diverse group of hybrids between mandarins and grapefruits or pummelos, the fruits vary tremendously. The colors range from pale yellow to deep orange, and the sizes from medium small to medium large. The flavors are quite distinctive, aromatic, and rich, often combining the best of both parents. Most varieties are best adapted to hot climates.

▋ **Tangor** This group of hybrids between mandarins and oranges includes 'Temple' and 'Murcott',

MANDARIN HYBRIDS – TANGELOS AND TANGORS

'Minneola' tangelo

'Orlando' tangelo

'Temple' tangor

which are thought to be naturally occurring hybrids, although their exact parentage is unknown.

The fruit flavor varies between orange and mandarin orange depending on the variety. The trees are about as hardy as orange trees and are slightly smaller.

▋ **Using mandarins** Mandarins, tangelos, and tangors range from sweet to tart; some are seedless and some are full of seeds; some are fairly large while others are tiny. They are easy to peel and have the distinctive mandarin flavor. All are most commonly eaten out of hand, but they also make excellent juice.

All varieties are best when they are heavy and full of juice. Avoid fruits that are extremely puffy, with soft spots. Mandarins are usually available in markets from November to May.

MANDARIN ORANGE AND HYBRIDS

Variety	Adaptation	Fruit description	Comments
'Calamondin'	CA, DS, FL, GC	Very small, few seeds, tender, juicy, acidic. Rind sweet and edible. Holds very well on tree.	Hybrid of mandarin and kumquat. Small columnar tree with small oval leaves. Productive and cold tolerant. Variegated form is also available.
'Changsha'	GC	Small to medium, early, seedy, good flavor. Resembles 'Satsuma'.	Very hardy; grown in cold areas of Gulf Coast. Bears early and true to type from seed.
'Clementine' ('Algerian')	CA, DS, FL, GC	Medium, early, few to many seeds, red-orange, sweet, juicy, fragrant, peels easily. Holds well on tree.	Small to medium tree with attractive weeping habit, dense foliage. Needs pollinator for best fruit production, but will be seedy. Many new, large-fruited strains becoming available.
'Dancy'	CA, DS, FL, GC	Medium, midseason, few to many seeds, richly flavored, acidic, peels and segments easily. Does not hold well on tree.	Medium to large, vigorous tree with few thorns. Traditional Christmas tangerine. Best in Florida.
'Encore'	CA, DS, FL, GC	Medium, late, tender, rich, juicy, colorful speckled rind peels easily. Holds well on tree.	Medium tree with many upright, spreading branches and few thorns. Tends to bear heavy crops in alternate years. Not widely available, but valuable for late-season fruit.
'Fairchild'	DS, GC	Medium, very early, many seeds, sweet, juicy. Holds fairly well on tree.	Medium, rounded, vigorous, nearly thornless tree. Best in low deserts of California and Arizona; requires heat.
'Honey'	CA, DS, FL, GC	Small, early, yellow-orange, many seeds, very sweet. Holds well on tree.	Medium to large, vigorous, spreading tree. Strong tendency for alternate bearing. Not widely available, but excellent flavor. The 'Honey' grown in Florida and the Gulf Coast is actually 'Murcott' (see Tangor 'Murcott').

MANDARIN ORANGE AND HYBRIDS

Variety	Adaptation	Fruit description	Comments
'Gold Nugget'	CA	Medium, late, light orange, seedless, rich, sweet flavor, often bumpy rind. Holds well on tree.	Medium, upright tree. Tendency for alternate bearing.
'Kara'	CA	Medium large, late, flavorful, remains tart until very mature. Holds fairly well on tree but becomes puffy.	Medium to large, thornless, moderately vigorous tree with drooping habit, and large dark green leaves. Best adapted to interior California.Tendency for alternate bearing.
'Kinnow'	CA, DS	Medium, midseason, juicy, seedy, richly flavored. Holds well on tree.	Large, frost-tolerant, vigorous, columnar tree with many long, slender, thornless branchlets. Attractive but strong tendency for alternate bearing.
'Mediterranean' ('Willowleaf')	CA, DS, FL, GC	Small to medium, midseason, seedy, juicy, sweet, aromatic, deteriorates quickly when mature. Fruit held toward inside of tree.	Small to medium, spreading tree with attractive small, narrow leaves, few thorns. Hardy but needs high heat for best fruit.
'Page'	CA, DS, FL, GC	Small to medium, early, few to many seeds, rich, sweet, excellent for juice. Holds well on tree.	Medium to large, very attractive tree with dense foliage, round top. Almost thornless. Somewhat alternate bearing.
'Pixie'	CA	Small to medium, midseason, light orange, seedless, sweet, bumpy rind, easy to peel.	Large, upright tree, good in milder areas. Tendency for alternate bearing.
'Satsuma'	CA, GC, FL	Medium, early, mild, sweet, low acid. Holds poorly on tree but stores well.	Small to medium, slow-growing, spreading tree with open, dark green foliage. Tough and very cold hardy. Popular in Northern California and Gulf Coast. 'Kimbrough' is a hardy 'Satsuma'-type mandarin for Gulf Coast.
'Seedless Kishu'	CA	Very small, early, often borne in clusters, seedless, excellent flavor, very loose rind easily removed. Holds reasonably well but rind puffs.	Small to medium tree. Easy-peeling, pop-in-the-mouth quality makes it a great snack fruit.
'Sunburst'	FL	Medium, early, seedy, mild, sweet, smooth bright orange-red rind.	Medium to large tree. Somewhat hardy. Tends to alternate bear.
'W. Murcott'	CA	Medium, late, flattened, excellent flavor, bright orange rind. Few seeds if grown without pollinator nearby, otherwise seedy. Fruit holds well on tree.	Medium tree. Tends to alternate bear. Often sold in supermarkets as 'Delite'. 'Tango' is a newer, seedless form.
'Yosemite Gold'	CA, DS	Large, midseason to late, deep orange-red, seedless, rich flavor, easy to peel.	Along with 'Shasta Gold' and 'Tahoe Gold', recent introduction from the University of California. Not widely tested.
Tangelo 'Minneola'	CA, DS, FL, GC	Large, late midseason, prominent nipple on top, rind reddish orange, flesh orange, few seeds, richly flavored, tart.	Medium to large, vigorous, attractive tree with large, pointed leaves, rounded habit. Best production with cross-pollination; not compatible with 'Orlando' tangelo.
Tangelo 'Orlando'	CA, DS, FL, GC	Medium to large, very early, orange rind and flesh, juicy, mildly sweet. Does not hold well on tree.	Medium to large tree. Leaves are distinctly cupped. Less vigorous and more cold tolerant than 'Minneola'. Needs pollinator for best production; not compatible with 'Minneola'.
Tangor 'Ortanique'	CA, DS, FL, GC	Medium size, late, flattened with smooth to bumpy bright orange rind. Aromatic, sweet, juicy. Usually seedy. Holds well.	Large tree. Jamaican variety becoming popular elsewhere.
Tangor 'Murcott' ('Murcott Honey')	FL	Medium, midseason to late, few to many seeds, rich, juicy, thin yellow-orange rind does not peel easily. Does not hold well on tree.	Tree medium in size and vigor, upright, very cold sensitive. Also classified as mandarin and sometimes sold as 'Honey', but origin unknown.
Tangor 'Temple'	DS, FL	Medium to large, midseason to late, seedy, rich, spicy. Holds fairly well on tree.	Small to medium, moderately vigorous, spreading, bushy tree. More sensitive to cold than mandarins and oranges.

Orange

Sweet orange types include blood, common, and navel oranges. Sour orange makes up a separate category.

■ **Blood orange** Under certain climatic conditions, a blood orange develops pink or red flesh, juice, and rind. Many people think its distinctive flavor, usually described as berrylike, is the most delicious of all the oranges.

Development of the red pigmentation is erratic and undependable. It is climate related, but the exact reasons for coloration are not completely understood. Color is intense some years, while in others there is no red pigmentation. Even fruits on the same tree vary.

Trees grown in the interior valleys of California produce fruits with the most consistent hue. 'Moro' develops the most consistent color in all areas. In Florida and along the Gulf Coast, color development is poor.

Tree size differs among blood orange varieties. 'Sanguinelli'

From left to right, comparison of 'Moro', 'Sanguinelli' and 'Tarocco' blood oranges

From left to right, 'Moro', 'Sanguinelli' and 'Tarocco' blood oranges in cross-section

'Moro' blood orange

'Sanguinelli' blood orange

'Tarocco' blood orange

BLOOD ORANGE

Variety	Adaptation	Fruit description	Comments
'Moro'	CA, DS	Medium, very early, juicy with distinctive aroma, almost seedless. Most consistent internal color. Flesh is violet or burgundy; rind is orange with pink blush. Holds well on tree but picks up musky flavor if left too long.	Medium, roundheaded, vigorous, spreading tree. Tends to bear heavily in alternate years. Fruit borne in clusters near outside of canopy, very attractive.
'Sanguinelli'	CA, DS	Small to medium, midseason to late, oblong, deep red rind, orange flesh with red streaks, few or no seeds, excellent flavor, very juicy. Holds well on tree.	Small to medium, almost thornless tree.
'Tarocco'	CA, DS	Medium to large, midseason, firm, juicy raspberry-flavor flesh, few seeds. Least reliable internal color. Does not hold well on tree.	Medium, moderately vigorous tree with open habit. Moderately productive, fruit held inside canopy. Best in interior California.

and 'Moro' are smaller and more compact than most other sweet oranges. 'Tarocco' is larger, growing to about the size of other sweet orange trees.

■ **Common orange** This type of orange is divided into two groups: those adapted to the Southwest and those adapted to the Southeast. 'Valencia', the most widely grown variety, is an exception. It is widely planted in both areas and throughout the commercial citrus areas of the world. Common oranges are typically used for fresh juice. The trees are generally about the same size as navel orange trees.

■ **Navel orange** The navel orange is distinguished by the presence of an undeveloped secondary fruit opposite the stem end. As this fruit enlarges it forms the small hole in the bottom of the fruit

known as the navel.

'Washington' is by far the most widely planted navel orange. The ease with which it peels and separates into segments and its crisp flesh make it the most popular dessert orange.

Navel oranges are genetically unstable. Mutations (sports) occur frequently, and they are often vegetatively propagated. Most are inferior to the 'Washington' navel, but several have been perpetuated because of their bright color or early bearing habit. 'Atwood', 'Fukamoto', 'Robertson', and 'Skaggs Bonanza' are sports commonly grown in California. Late-ripening navels, such as 'Lane Late', are also becoming more popular. These varieties can extend the navel orange harvest into early summer. 'Dream', 'Glen',

'Valencia' sweet orange

and 'Surprise' are sometimes grown in Florida and Texas, where they may perform better than 'Washington'.

All navel oranges are best adapted to intermediate climates

COMMON ORANGE

Variety	Adaptation	Fruit description	Comments
'Diller'	DS	Medium, early, sweet, juicy, few to many seeds. Excellent juice orange. Holds well on tree.	Small to medium, moderately vigorous tree with short, upright branches. Well adapted to the desert, above-average cold tolerance.
'Hamlin'	DS, FL, GC	Small to medium, very early, usually seedless, well colored. Tender and juicy but low acidity.	Medium to large, moderately vigorous tree bears heavy crop. Produces small fruit in desert. Tolerates cold, but less resistant to injury than 'Parson'.
'Marrs'	FL, GC	Medium to large, very early, few to many seeds. Juicy, sweet fruit lacks acid, but quality improves if harvest is delayed to later in season.	Small tree, moderately vigorous, bears prolifically at an early age. Fruit is borne in clusters near outside of tree.
'Midsweet'	FL, GC	Medium, midseason, moderately seedy, darker juice than 'Pineapple'.	Medium size tree. Slightly later and hardier than 'Pineapple'.
'Parson' ('Parson Brown')	FL, GC	Medium to large, very early, seedy, juicy, sweet. Popular juice orange.	Large, upright, vigorous tree bears heavy crop. Relatively cold tolerant. Best adapted to Florida.
'Pineapple'	FL, GC	Medium, midseason, richly flavored fruit named for its delicate fragrance. Moderately seedy, well colored but does not hold well on tree.	Medium to large, moderately vigorous, thornless tree tends to bear heavy crops in alternate years. Sensitive to frost.
'Shamouti' ('Palestine Jaffa')	CA, DS, GC	Large, midseason, nearly seedless, firm, fragrantly sweet, peels and sections easily. Popular eating orange in Europe.	Medium, nearly thornless tree with upright habit and dense foliage. 'Washington' navel is better in the United States.
'Trovita'	CA, DS	Small to medium, midseason to late, juicy, pleasant flavor, few seeds.	Tall, upright, vigorous tree bears fruit within dense, dark green foliage. Well adapted to desert as well as cool coastal California. Tends toward alternate bearing. Probably originated as seedling of 'Washington' navel but lacks navel on fruit.
'Valencia'	CA, DS, FL, GC	Medium to large, late, usually seedy, very juicy, sweet or slightly acid in cool climates. Rind may regreen in summer but quality is unaffected. Holds very well on tree.	Large, upright tree tends toward alternate bearing of heavy crops. Very wide range of adaptation. 'Midnight' and 'Delta' are earlier, seedless forms.

Orange *(continued)*

(neither too hot and dry nor too cold and wet) of California.

Standard navel orange trees reach 16 to 20 feet high; sports are smaller and slower growing.

'Washington' navel (left) and 'Cara Cara' pink navel (right)

■ **Sour orange** The sour orange is not widely grown for its fruit, which is bitter. The fruit is used to make orange marmalade and various liqueurs. The tree is often used as an ornamental for its clean foliage, brightly colored fruit, and fragrant flowers. The varieties 'Bouquet de Fleurs' and 'Chinotto' are especially useful in the landscape because of their distinctive foliage and compact growth habit.

■ **Using sweet oranges** For the cook the seedy blood orange does not have the versatility of seedless common and navel oranges, and it also lacks the piquant flavor of sour orange. But the bright red flesh, especially the dark crimson of 'Moro', makes a lasting impression even if served merely squeezed and strained into a clear juice glass. Cut into wedges or sliced, blood orange makes a dramatic garnish on fish dishes, atop creamed soups, in salads, and on dull dinner plates. Maltaise sauce, a variation on lemon-flavored hollandaise sauce, is made with the juice and zest of blood orange. A tart made with the thickened juice of a dark blood orange, or an ice made with the juice and a bit of zest, is unforgettable.

'Cara Cara' navel orange

'Washington' navel orange

'Lane Late' navel orange

NAVEL ORANGE

Variety	Adaptation	Fruit description	Comments
'Cara Cara'	CA, DS, FL, GC	Large, early, with excellent-flavored, salmon-pink flesh. Seedless. Holds well.	Sport of 'Washington' navel discovered in Venezuela. Called red navel in Southeast. Color fades as season progresses.
'Lane Late'	CA, DS	Similar to 'Washington' navel but slightly smaller and several weeks later. Holds very well.	'Washington' navel bud sport from Australia. Extends navel season into summer.
'Robertson'	CA, DS	Identical to 'Washington' navel except the fruit is smaller and borne in tight clusters near outside of tree.	Bud sport of 'Washington' navel. The tree is smaller and more heat resistant, and fruit ripens 10 to 14 days earlier than the parent. Fruit considered inferior to 'Washington' navel.
'Summernavel'	CA	Large, flavorful fruit similar to 'Washington' navel but with thicker, rougher rind. Fruit matures later than 'Washington', holds well on tree.	Bud sport of 'Washington' navel, but tree is more vigorous, low, and spreading. Also has larger leaves than parent.
'Washington'	CA, DS, FL, GC	Large, flavorful, seedless, moderately juicy, peels and sections easily. Ripens early, holds well on tree.	Medium tree with round top. Best in interior California. Drops fruit in dry, hot areas. The original and still the best navel variety.

The essential oil of common and navel oranges is used to flavor custards, creams, doughs, stews, soups, pastries, and cookies. Add the flavor of orange flower water and the odor of 'Bergamot' and you will find the scent of sweet orange at every turn.

Whereas the oils of orange zest (the thin, pigmented portion of the rind) can permeate a dish, the flesh of the sweet orange (including seedless navel orange) can be a subtle complement or foil for foods with a wide variety of textures and flavors. Remove the pith, seeds, and pips (small, undeveloped seeds) from a sweet orange, slice it thinly, and serve it with black olives; with thinly sliced raw fennel bulb, purple onion, radishes, or daikon; or with watercress or other bitter greens, and a mild vinaigrette. The combinations make a complex salad course. Or serve the slices chilled and sprinkled with orange-flavored liqueur and finely granulated sugar in a traditional salade d'orange. Nothing could be more refreshing.

Serve chilled sweet orange juice as a beverage in itself, or use it as an ingredient in a liquid concoction. Seeded sweet orange varieties are especially rich and juicy, and the seeds can be strained out easily. In winter make hot mulled wine with a little orange juice, dry red wine, cinnamon sticks, cloves, sugar,

'Bergamot' sour orange

'Chinotto' sour orange

'Bouquet de Fleurs' sour orange

'Bouquet de Fleurs' sour orange flower

orange and lemon slices, and a drop of angostura bitters. In summer serve a pitcher of iced sangria made with sweetened orange juice, a nice burgundy, soda, and orange slices.

■ **Using sour orange** Though well known throughout the Western world, sour oranges are not usually available at the produce market, perhaps because

they make a tart juice and are sour to eat out of hand. But for marmalade no other orange can compare. Sour orange supplies a much more pungent, tart orange flavor than any sweet orange. Sour orange is rich in pectin (the pith of oranges is one of the sources of commercial pectin) and acid. It is easy to make a fine marmalade without adding any pectin.

SOUR ORANGE

Variety	Adaptation	Fruit description	Comments
'Bergamot'	CA	Medium to large with light green to yellow, bumpy rind. Very seedy.	Aromatic rind oils used in perfumes and colognes and to flavor Earl Grey tea. Attractive small to medium, spreading tree. Considered a lime–sour orange hybrid. Not cold hardy.
'Bouquet' ('Bouquet de Fleurs')	CA, DS, FL, GC	Small to medium, deep orange fruit follows large clusters of very aromatic flowers.	Small, spreading, thornless tree has dense clusters of rounded, ruffled, deep green leaves. Ideal hedge, container, or specimen plant.
'Chinotto' ('Myrtle-Leaf Orange')	CA, DS, FL, GC	Small, flattened, deep orange fruit is held in clusters almost year-round.	Blooms profusely. Small, round, thornless tree has dense, compact habit, small, pointed, dark green leaves. Good hedge or container plant.
'Seville'	CA, DS, FL, GC	Medium, flattened, very sour; used in marmalade in England.	Medium, thorny, upright, vigorous tree useful for patio, street-side, and specimen plantings. Very hardy.

Pummelo

Sometimes called shaddock, pummelo is often two to three times larger than grapefruit. It is popular in Asia but has only recently caught the eye of American gardeners. Varieties with white or pink flesh are available. 'Chandler', a pink variety, is the most widely available. Its flesh is moderately juicy, with a sweet, aromatic flavor, and its rind is yellow, thick, and smooth. The fruit is borne on a large, open, vigorous tree with big woody flowers. It needs hot summers for best fruit production and flavor.

Pummelo has a thick peel.

Some varieties, such as 'Tahitian' ('Sarawak'), African shaddock, and red shaddock, may be available locally in Florida and California.

Most pummelos are large spreading trees that grow 15 to 18 feet high and wide. The fruit is produced in clusters among the huge deep green leaves.

■ **Using pummelo** The fruit can create quite a stir at the table, if only because of its huge dimensions. Although pummelo looks like a large grapefruit, most varieties are sweeter and less acidic than grapefruit, with a thicker peel and firmer, less juicy flesh. The sections are sometimes irregular, creating a mosaic pattern when halved. Pummelo is best eaten peeled and segmented, with the membranes removed.

Because the fruit is not widely grown commercially, it appears in markets for only a few months after the first of the year despite the fact that it matures at the same time as grapefruit. Choose heavier (juicier) fruit with solid yellow skin.

'Chandler' pummelos can weigh up to several pounds each.

Citrus relatives

The citrus family is huge, with many types and varieties not yet widely available in the United States.

▌ **Rare citrus** These include low-acid fruits such as sweet lemon (*Citrus limetta*) and sweet lime (*C. limettioides*), which are popular in Mexico and the Near East, as well as tart fruits such as yuzu (*C. junos*) and sudachi (*C. sudachi*), which are favorites in some areas of Asia. You may be able to find these unusual citrus fruits in local specialty markets. Many citrus relatives are exceptionally handsome plants that are useful in the landscape.

▌ **Orange jessamine** (*Murraya paniculata*) With its small, dense, shiny green leaves the plant makes an excellent hedge. Clusters of powerfully fragrant white flowers are followed by inedible bright red fruit. Hardy to about 25°F, the shrub grows 5 to 15 feet high.

▌ **Wampi** (*Clausena lansium*) The plant, which grows to about 25 feet high, has coarser texture than most other members of the citrus family. Its large white flower clusters are followed by small, edible yellowish brown fruit.

▌ **Trifoliate orange** (*Poncirus trifoliata*) Although not the most

Sweet lemon, *Citrus limetta*, is more common in India and the Mediterranean than in North America.

beautiful member of the citrus family, trifoliate orange is a hardy, deciduous plant that can be grown in cold climates as far north as Washington, D.C. Its growth is thorny and its fruit is seedy and acidic, but it makes an effective barrier or hedge. The variety 'Flying Dragon', which shows great promise as a dwarfing rootstock, makes an attractive bonsai or container plant.

Orange jessamine, *Murraya paniculata*, is a compact citrus relative that makes a handsome hedge or container plant.

Wampi, *Clausena lansium*, bears clusters of white blossoms which develop into small edible fruits.

Trifoliate orange, *Poncirus trifoliata*, is a hardy, thorny, deciduous tree most often used as a rootstock.

THE BEST SUBTROPICAL FRUITS

Subtropical fruits vary widely in flavor, landscape value, and growing requirements. Use this chapter to help you choose the best species and varieties for your garden. The following encyclopedia describes more than 50 subtropical fruits. (Chapter 5, beginning on page 38, provides information about citrus fruits.)

Each of the major fruit descriptions contains a quick reference fact box. Also included is a map showing the areas where the plant is well adapted (red) and marginally adapted (yellow). In marginal areas choose hardy varieties if they are available and plant them in protected areas. It's important to remember that these maps are for quick reference only. You'll find more precise information in the "Adaptation" section of each fruit description and in Chapter 2, "Understanding Climate", beginning on page 8.

■ **Entry details** The information in the text following the quick-reference fact list includes descriptions of the plant's growth habit, harvest season, ornamental quality, and suitability for container culture. The descriptions also include information on adaptation, pollination, propagation, site selection, watering, fertilizing, pruning, pest and disease control, and harvesting and storing. All the subtropical fruits described in this book are available from one or more nursery sources, but some varieties will be harder to find than others. You may need to contact several nurseries to find the one you want.

■ **Harvest periods** The harvest periods listed in the fruit descriptions are only general guidelines. To adapt these guidelines to your area, remember that fruit ripens earlier in warmer areas than in cooler locations. Adjust the expected harvest date accordingly.

■ **New flavors** Some of the fruits described in this chapter are undeniably delicious. Mango, papaya, cherimoya, and many others—although perhaps new to you— will be an absolute pleasure to eat.

Some of the subtropical fruits, such as tree tomato and passionfruit, may seem a bit unusual at first. You may find them more palatable in preserves or used in cooking. The important thing is to give yourself time to enjoy these fruits and to experiment with new ways to use them.

■ **Selected varieties** Most plants grown from seed are genetically unique, different in major or minor ways from all other plants of the same species. They may have better fruit quality, a different plant habit, a wider range of adaptation, or a darker leaf. These differences are the basis of natural selection. In their native habitats plants that possess certain advantages are better competitors and are more likely to survive.

In horticulture plants that have desirable characteristics are vegetatively propagated and called cultivars (short for "cultivated variety"). Selected varieties of each subtropical fruit, if any, are listed in the charts with each plant description. Unless a plant breeds true from seed, cultivars should always be your first choice. When you purchase a cultivar, you are assured it will have the superior fruit quality or the specific adaptations of its parent.

■ **Pollination** The pollination requirements of subtropical fruits deserve special attention. Species and varieties that set fruit without another tree nearby are called self-fruitful. These plants either provide their own pollen or else their flowers do not require pollination to set fruit. Species or varieties that must be pollinated by another, different variety are called self-sterile, self-unfruitful, or incompatible. In the absence of natural pollinators, such as bees or flies, some fruits must be hand pollinated. This is usually the case with cherimoya and can be a problem with many plants grown in greenhouses, where insect access may be limited. The specific pollination requirements of each fruit are included in the encyclopedia.

If space is limited consider grafting a pollinator limb onto a tree rather than planting two trees. For more about grafting, see pages 28–30.

◄ **Cherimoya, avocado, baby red banana, lychee, kiwifruit, golden kiwifruit, lime, papaya, mango, pineapple, passionfruit, oranges, and bananas are among the many subtropical fruits you can grow and enjoy.**

GALLERY OF SUBTROPICAL PLANTS

Avocado

Alligator pear, love fruit
Persea americana

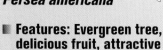

- **Features:** Evergreen tree, delicious fruit, attractive foliage
- **Size:** 20–60'H×25–35'W
- **Hardiness:** 18°–32°F
- **Harvest:** Depends on variety

The seedcoat of an avocado becomes papery when the fruit is mature.

The avocado is generally a large, dominating tree that, under the proper conditions, provides an abundant harvest of rich, buttery, delicious fruit.

Native to tropical Central America and Mexico, three races of avocado are in cultivation—Mexican, Guatemalan, and West Indian—as well as hybrids of these groups. Mexican and Guatemalan types and hybrids of the two are best adapted to California and moderately cold areas of Central Florida. West Indian hybrids are best adapted to South Florida and Hawaii. Although there are great similarities among groups, Mexican varieties are generally hardier and bear fruit with a smooth, thin skin that is shiny green or purplish-black. Guatemalan avocados do best in relatively frost-free climates and bear dark green fruit with a thick, bumpy rind. West Indian varieties are the most frost sensitive and have thin, smooth, green to greenish yellow skin.

Avocado fruits vary from round to pear-shape, depending on the variety. They may be as small as 4 ounces or as large as 2 pounds. Because these varieties ripen at different times of the year, avocados are almost always available in the supermarket.

An avocado tree can become quite large under ideal growing conditions and may live 100 or more years. It is a stately tree when used as a single specimen but is generally too large for a small garden. A productive dwarf or semidwarf variety is better suited to small gardens. The mature foliage is deep green and leathery. Coppery red new growth appears in flushes throughout the growing season. The leaves of Mexican varieties have a scent like anise. Avocado's flowers, borne in clusters, are yellowish white.

The fruits of the many avocado varieties differ in flavor. A high oil content usually means rich flavor.

- **Adaptation** Avocados are widely grown in the mild-winter areas of Florida, California, South Texas, and Hawaii. Some hardier varieties can also be grown in cooler parts of coastal and inland California and in coastal North Florida.

Although the foliage of the hardiest Mexican varieties can withstand temperatures as low as 18°F, the fruit and flowers are less hardy and will be damaged at 32°F. Cool weather during bloom can limit fruit set, and high

Avocado leaves are shiny deep green. Their dense arrangement on the tree casts deep shade.

temperatures after fruit set may cause excessive fruit drop.

Lack of adequate soil drainage is often the most important limiting factor in growing avocado. Poorly drained soils or constantly wet soils conducive to root rot can kill a tree.

Pollination Most avocados are at least partially self-fruitful, and in ideal climates there are usually enough neighborhood trees to provide for pollination and adequate crops. However, by combining the right varieties you can increase yields. Avocado flowers are classed as type A or B. Varieties with type A flowers are receptive to pollen in the morning but don't release their pollen until the afternoon of the following day. The situation is reversed with Type B avocados: The flowers are receptive in the afternoon, but the pollen isn't released until the following morning. Combining varieties with different flower types ensures that plenty of pollen is available when flowers are most receptive and results in high yields, although a single tree will produce enough fruit for most families.

If space is limited, either graft a pollenizer limb onto the primary desired variety or plant more than one tree in a single hole. Semidwarf varieties are also useful in small gardens.

'Mexicola' bears smooth, purple-skinned fruits on hardy trees adapted to California growing conditions.

AVOCADO VARIETIES FOR CALIFORNIA

Variety*	Fruit description	Ripening season	Comments
'Anaheim' (A)	Large to very large, green, fair flavor.	June–Aug	Fairly small, upright tree. Very productive. Hardy to 30°F.
'Bacon' (B)	Medium, thin green skin, good flavor.	Oct–Mar	Medium, upright tree. Very productive. Hardy to 24°F.
'Fuerte' (B)	Small to medium, thin green skin, excellent flavor.	Nov–Mar	Large, spreading tree. Production somewhat erratic. Hardy to 28°F.
'Hass' (A)	Small to medium, thick purple to black skin, excellent nutty flavor.	Feb–Oct	Medium to large tree. Alternate bearing. Hardy to 30°F. 'Lamb Hass' bears more, slightly larger fruit.
'Mexicola' (A)	Small, thin purple skin, very good nutty flavor.	Aug–Oct	Medium, spreading tree. Heavy producer. Hardy to 18°F.
'Nabal' (B)	Medium, medium green skin, excellent flavor.	June–Oct	Large, upright tree. Erratic but heavy producer. Hardy to 30°F.
'Pinkerton' (A)	Small to medium, thick green skin, very good flavor.	Oct–Jan	Medium, slightly spreading tree. Heavy producer. Hardy to 30°F.
'Reed' (A)	Medium to large, thick green skin, excellent flavor.	June–Nov	Medium, upright tree. Heavy producer. Hardy to 30°F.
'Stewart' (B)	Small to medium, thin dark purple skin, great flavor.	Oct–Jan	Compact, medium-size tree. Hardy to 24°F.
'Zutano' (B)	Medium, thin green skin, good flavor.	Dec–Jan	Large tree. Heavy producer. Hardy to 26°F.

*Letter in parentheses indicates flower type (see "Pollination" above)

Avocado *(continued)*

'Reed' avocado bears thick-skinned green fruits over a long harvest season.

avocados. See pages 29–30 for the techniques.

Older, established trees can be topworked, a method where shoots of a new variety are grafted onto the main branches or trunk of a mature tree.

▮ Site selection and planting Plant an avocado in well-drained soil in an area with full sun. The tree will not tolerate standing water, and it has a low tolerance for saline (salty) soil. A pH of 5.5 to 6.5 is ideal. With proper fertilization it tolerates more alkaline conditions. Choose a site at least 25 feet from a building or power lines, where the tree will have room to spread.

Spring is the best time to plant an avocado. Position the tree so its crown is slightly higher than it was in the nursery container to allow for settling.

▮ Avocado in the landscape A large and dense tree, avocado casts heavy shade and regularly drops leaves. It can be used as a background tree, specimen, or screen but is not well-adapted to small gardens and is not a good tree to garden under. Dwarf varieties, such as 'Wurtz', are

▮ Propagation The seed from an avocado fruit will usually germinate. It can take years, however, before a seedling bears fruit, and the quality will probably be inferior to that of the fruit of the parent tree. Seedlings can be used as rootstocks for grafting your own tree unless you live in an area where avocado root rot is a problem. In such locales you're better off planting varieties grafted to root rot–resistant rootstocks, such as 'Duke 7', but even that won't ensure success.

Seedlings are ready to graft when they reach ¼ to ⅜ inch in diameter. Obtain budwood from dormant terminal growth (shoot tips that are not actively growing), which is just starting to swell in the spring. Remove the leaves to keep the wood from drying out.

Chip and shield budding are common methods for propagating

'Hass' is one of the most popular avocados in California.

more versatile and can be grown in smaller spaces as well as in large containers.

Caring for avocado

Watering The most important aspect of growing avocado successfully is careful watering. As is usually the case with plants that are sensitive to soil moisture levels, too much water is as dangerous as not enough. Feeder roots, the ones most sensitive to overly wet soil, are concentrated in the top 15 inches of soil. Allow this zone to dry partially before watering a mature tree. An avocado tree will survive with less water, but for a quality harvest in dry climates, you will probably have to water deeply every two to four weeks. A young tree will need more frequent watering, probably every week or two depending on the weather.

Use a basin to direct water to the root zone, making sure to increase the size of the basin as the tree grows. Occasional deep watering will help leach salts from the soil. Break the walls of the basin to provide drainage during a rainy season. An organic mulch, 3 to 6 inches deep and kept several inches away from the trunk, will help prevent phytophthora root rot and keep the feeder roots cool.

Fertilizing From early spring to late summer, apply only small amounts of a complete fertilizer. A young tree that is growing slowly can be fed with a complete fertilizer such as Miracle-Gro Shake 'n Feed Continuous Release Citrus, Avocado & Mango Plant Food. In colder climates do not fertilize a tree after late summer to reduce the chance of late-season growth that will not become cold hardy.

Avocado grown in high-pH soil often shows signs of iron deficiency (interveinal yellowing of new growth). Correct the deficiency with applications of iron chelate.

Pruning An avocado tree requires little work other than shaping when it is young and removing dead or misplaced branches as it matures. It can, however, be pruned regularly to keep it within bounds. A fully

'Pinkerton' is a medium-size avocado with very good flavor.

AVOCADO VARIETIES FOR FLORIDA

Variety*	Fruit description	Ripening season	Comments
'Booth 7' (B)	Medium to large, green, good flavor.	Oct–Dec	Medium, spreading tree. Hardy to 25–30°F.
'Brogdin' (A-B)	Small to medium, dark purple, very good flavor, difficult to peel.	July–Sept	Medium, upright tree. Good for colder areas. Hardy to 22°F.
'Choquette' (A)	Large to very large, green, very good flavor.	Nov–Feb	Medium, spreading tree resists scab disease. Hardy to 26°F.
'Donnie' (A)	Large, green, very mild but bland flavor.	May–June	Bland flavor; popular because of its earliness. Hardy to 30°F.
'Hall' (B)	Large to very large, green, good flavor.	Nov–Feb	Medium tree. Heavy producer. Hardy to 28°F.
'Lula' (A)	Medium to large, green, good flavor.	Nov–Feb	Large, upright, tough tree. Also popular in South Texas. Hardy to 25°F.
'Miguel' (B)	Large, green, excellent quality.	Aug–Sept	Medium tree. Very, productive. Hardy to 30°F.
'Monroe' (B)	Large, green, good flavor.	Nov–Jan	Medium tree. Hardy to 26°F.
'Pollock' (B)	Large to very large, green, very good flavor.	July–Sept	Medium, spreading tree resists scab disease. Light producer. Hardy to 30°F.
'Russell' (A)	Large, gourd shape, green, fair flavor.	July–Sept	Small- to medium-size tree. Hardy to 30°F.
'Simmonds' (A)	Large to very large, green, very good flavor.	July–Sept	Medium, spreading tree resists scab disease. Heavy producer. Hardy to 30°F.

*Letter in parentheses indicates flower type (see "Pollination" on page 65)

Avocado *(continued)*

mature avocado tree can be cut back to a 3-foot stump (make sure to cut above the graft union); it will usually bear fruit again in three years. If you try this technique, select the strongest of the new shoots and remove any weak growth or misplaced branches. The new shoots may need staking to prevent them from breaking in strong winds.

■ **Pests and diseases** Avocado root rot (phytophthora) is a major disease problem in California and low-lying areas of Florida. Select certified disease-free plants and avoid planting where soil drainage is poor or flooding occurs. The disease is easily transported by equipment, tools, and shoes from infected soil to uninfected soil. Once a tree is infected (signs include yellowing and dropping leaves), there is little you can do but cut back on water. Deep mulching with 6 to 12 inches

of organic matter such as bark chips (keep the mulch 6 to 12 inches away from the trunk) and regular applications of gypsum (25 pounds per year per tree) can help suppress avocado root rot. Planting on a 2- to 3-foot-tall mound improves drainage and helps prevent the disease.

In the humid Southeast and Hawaii, fungus diseases such as scab, anthracnose, and powdery mildew are common. Check with your local cooperative extension service for control measures. Scale insects, loopers, borers, and thrips may attack avocados, but they are usually not serious enough to require chemical control. Snails and persea mites also can be problems on trees in California.

■ **Harvest and storage** Knowing exactly when to pick an avocado can be tricky. The length of time from pollination to harvest differs according to variety. 'Fuerte'

'Gwen' avocado has small fruits.

AVOCADO VARIETIES FOR HAWAII

Variety*	Fruit description	Ripening season	Comments
'Case' (B)	Medium to large, green, very good flavor.	Dec–Feb	Medium tree. Good producer.
'Chang' (B)	Medium to large, green, very good flavor.	Mar–Aug	Medium tree. Consistently heavy producer.
'Greengold' (A)	Medium to large, thick green skin, excellent nutty flavor.	Jan–Apr	Medium, spreading tree. Heavy producer.
'Hayes' (A)	Medium to large, purple, very good flavor.	Jan–Apr	Medium tree, good producer. Susceptible to mites.
'Kahaluu' (B)	Medium to large, thin green skin, excellent flavor.	Aug–Oct	Medium to large, upright tree. Light producer. Susceptible to thrips and mites.
'Malama' ('Purple Kaha') (B)	Medium, purple, rich nutty flavor, low fiber.	Oct–Feb	Productive.
'Murashige' (B)	Large, thick dark green skin, small seed, excellent flavor.	May–July	Medium, upright, handsome tree. Tends to bear heavily in alternate years. Short storage life.
'Nishikawa' (B)	Medium to very large, thick green skin, very good flavor.	Dec–Apr	Medium tree. Good producer.
'Ohata' (A)	Large to very large, thick purple skin, very good flavor.	Mar–Aug	Medium tree. Light producer.
'San Miguel' (A)	Small to medium, thin purple skin, excellent flavor.	Sept–Nov	Productive.
'Sharwil' (B)	Small to medium, thin green skin, excellent flavor.	Dec–Apr	Medium, spreading tree. Bears heavily in alternate years.
'Yamagata' (B)	Medium to large, green, small seed, good flavor.	Mar–July	Consistent bearing.

*Letter in parentheses indicates flower type (see "Pollination" on page 65)

needs 8 to 10 months under ideal conditions, but 'Hass' requires 13 to 14 months. The fruit of some varieties can be stored on the tree for 9 to 20 weeks without losing flavor and quality. Other varieties have a shorter period (from 6 to 8 weeks) of peak flavor. Overly mature fruit will soften on the tree and develop an off flavor. In hot summer months the fruit matures more quickly than in cooler winter months. In any case the fruit must be picked when mature but still hard, and ripened off the tree. Immature fruit will wrinkle, won't soften evenly, and will have poor flavor.

Dark varieties begin to turn from green to black when they are ready to be picked. Green varieties develop a yellowish tinge. When you think the crop is beginning to ripen, pick one of the larger fruits and allow it to ripen in a paper bag with a banana or an apple. A ripe fruit feels soft under gentle pressure. Remove the flesh and check the seedcoat, a thin membrane that covers the seed. A dark brown, paper-thin seedcoat is a good sign of a mature fruit. An immature fruit has a light tan or yellow seedcoat.

Use handheld pruning shears to harvest the fruit, leaving a small piece of stem attached to help prevent decay during ripening or storage. For tall trees you'll probably need a ladder or collapsible extension fruit harvester, available in many garden centers.

■ **Avocado at the table** If you are an avocado fancier, you know how wonderful a ripe avocado is

Some avocados turn black when ripe.

simply halved; sprinkled with salt, pepper, and lime juice; and eaten with a spoon. For a more elegant presentation, fan slices on a bed of greens with various fruits, garnish with capers, and dress with a vinaigrette. Remember that a cut avocado browns rapidly. Coat sliced fruit with lemon or lime juice to prevent discoloration.

Guacamole is probably the most popular avocado dish. There are many versions of guacamole, but most are made of avocados mashed with bits of ripe tomato, lime juice, salt, hot red pepper flakes, cumin, chopped cilantro, and minced onion. Serve guacamole with tortilla chips or raw vegetables, or use it to garnish bowls of chili, enchiladas, or turkey sandwiches.

'Zutano' is a hardier variety of avocado well adapted to California.

DWARF AVOCADO VARIETIES FOR CONTAINERS AND SMALL GARDENS**

Variety* (flower type)	Fruit description	Ripening season	Comments
'Gwen' (A)	Small, medium green skin, excellent flavor.	Mar–Nov	Small, compact, upright tree to 12–14' high. Heavy producer. Hardy to 28–30°F.
'Whitsell' (B)	Small, thick green skin, excellent flavor.	Mar–July	Small, compact tree to 12' high. Bears heavily in alternate years. Hardy to 28–30°F.
'Wurtz' ('Wertz', 'Little Cado') (A)	Small, thick green skin, good flavor.	May–Sept	Very small, compact tree reaches 8–10' high. Light producer. Hardy to 28–30°F.

*Letter in parentheses indicates flower type (see "Pollination" on page 65)
**Available primarily in California.

Banana

Musa acuminata and M. balbisiana hybrids

- **Features:** Huge leaves, exotic flowers, delicious fruit
- **Size:** 2–25'H×spreading clump
- **Hardiness:** Foliage 32°F, rhizomes 22°F
- **Harvest:** 12–18 months after planting, 4–8 months after flowering

Bananas and their relatives are staple foods for most tropical countries. There are many species of banana, but the edible types were developed by crossing and recrossing two species: *Musa acuminata*, a sweet banana, and *M. balbisiana*, a starchier banana that is more vigorous and resistant to disease. Most of the commonly available varieties are seedless hybrids of the two species that usually resemble one parent more than the other. For instance, the finest bananas for fresh eating, such as 'Cavendish', resemble *M. acuminata*. Cooking bananas, commonly called plantains, are closer to *M. balbisiana*.

Banana plants are extremely decorative, ranking next to palm trees for the wonderful tropical feeling they lend to the landscape. Technically they are

Bananas provide excellent screening.

The large leaves of bananas provide superb tropical ambience.

herbaceous perennials arising from underground stems called rhizomes. The fleshy stalks sheathed with huge, broad leaves can rise 5 to 25 feet in as little as six months, depending on the variety. Each stalk produces one large flower cluster, which develops fruit and then dies. New stalks grow from the rhizome. Fruit size and flavor vary considerably, but most home garden varieties are 4 to 8 inches long and very sweet. The clusters of fruit may weigh more than 100 pounds.

Adaptation The plants grow best in a uniformly warm climate and require 10 to 15 months of frost-free conditions to produce a flower stalk. The fruit takes four to eight months to mature, depending on the temperature. All but the hardiest varieties stop growing when the temperature drops below 50°F.

Freezing temperatures will kill banana leaves. Prolonged temperatures below 28°F will kill the plant to the ground. However, if the temperature does not fall below 22°F and the cold period is short, the rhizome will usually survive and resprout when the weather warms.

The ideal temperature for ripening fruit is around 80°F. A plant grows slowly above that point and stops growing entirely at 100°F. High temperatures and bright sunlight will scorch the leaves and fruit.

In most areas banana requires wind protection for best appearance and maximum yield. The heavy fruit clusters, large leaves, and shallow roots make tall plants susceptible to being blown over. Wind also tatters the leaves.

Pollination The banana fruit develops without pollination. The plant produces a long flower

'Dwarf Red' banana has attractive red stems and bears tasty fruit.

Bananas and palms are natural tropical partners.

A banana plant in a large pot becomes garden art.

stalk with rows of female flowers called hands. The fruit, or fingers, begin to develop at the base of the stalk (closest to where it originates on the plant). The developing fruits point downward under a protective sheath at first. When the sheath falls off and the fruits begin to grow, they curve upward.

The male flowers don't appear until all the fruits have begun to grow. Although pretty, they take energy from the plant. For this reason commercial banana growers cut the flower stalk off just below the last hand.

Propagation Banana is usually propagated by division. See page 31 for more detail.

Site selection and planting Banana is usually sold as semidormant rhizomes or as container-grown suckers. Find a protected planting spot in full sun. If you purchased rhizomes, plant them close to the surface of a deep, well-drained soil rich in organic matter and with a pH between 5.5 and 6.5. Plant suckers at the same depth that they grew previously. Banana is not tolerant of salty soils.

Banana in the landscape Big beautiful leaves evoke visions of tropical climes regardless of whether the plant produces fruit. Fast-growing and upright, larger varieties can be used as background plants, privacy screens, or specimens. Smaller types are perfect for containers and can be grown indoors in bright light. Those with variegated or colored foliage provide a perfect

accent. Bananas are unbeatable for creating tropical ambiance.

Caring for banana

Watering The huge leaves of a banana plant use a great deal of water. Regular, deep watering is absolutely necessary during warm weather. Do not let plants dry out, but don't overwater; standing water, especially in cool weather, causes root rot. Spread a thick layer of mulch on the soil to conserve moisture, retard weeds, and protect the shallow roots.

In dry-summer regions, such as Southern California, use extra water occasionally to leach out the accumulated soil salts.

Fertilizing Its rapid growth rate makes banana a heavy feeder. During warm weather apply a balanced fertilizer once a month. A mature plant may require as much as 1 to 2 pounds monthly of a 6 percent nitrogen fertilizer. A young plant needs one-quarter to one-third as much. In many areas bananas also benefit from micronutrients.

Spread the fertilizer evenly around the plant in a circle extending 4 to 8 feet from the trunk. Do not allow the fertilizer to touch the trunk.

Pruning Allow only one primary stem on each rhizome to fruit. Remove excess shoots as soon as you notice them so that the plant will channel more energy into fruit production. (Some growers prefer to allow six to eight suckers to develop, in the belief that the extra

suckers nourish the clump and provide more selection options for replacement). Once the main stalk is six to eight months old, permit one sucker to develop as a replacement stalk for the following season.

After harvesting the fruit cut the stalk back to 30 inches above the ground. Remove the stub several weeks later. Dispose of the cut stems to prevent disease.

Pests and diseases Banana has few troublesome pests or diseases outside tropical regions. The best way to avoid problems is to purchase disease-free plants from a reputable source and plant them in a well-drained soil. The soilborne disease banana wilt, sigatoka fungal foliar diseases, nematodes, and various weevils can be problems in Florida and other warm, humid climates. For control measures consult your cooperative extension service.

Dwarf bananas are perfect for small pots on the patio.

Banana *(continued)*

'Praying Hands' banana has unique clustered hands.

A banana cluster may have more than 100 fingers.

'Dwarf Brazilian' banana

'Ice Cream' banana

■ Harvest and storage Fruit carried on the plant through winter will mature quickly when warmer weather arrives. If you live in a cool area, you may want to cover the clusters with plastic or brown paper to increase the temperature of the fruit and hasten maturity. Covering the fruit can also help prevent sunburn and other blemishes. Leave the bottom of the cover open to prevent moisture buildup. Some clusters may need staking to support the weight of developing fruits.

The fruit must ripen off the plant because it will usually split if left on after maturity. A banana acquires most of its nutrients and sugars in the three to four weeks prior to maturity, however, so it is important not to pick too early. When hands at the top of the stalk begin to turn yellow, it's time to cut the entire stalk.

You can store a mature stalk of bananas at 55°F for one to two weeks. Temperatures below 50°F injure bananas, so don't put them in the refrigerator. The fruit will ripen in several days at room temperature.

■ Banana at the table Banana is a favorite for fresh eating. You'll be amazed at how flavorful homegrown bananas can be. They are excellent in fruit salads, pies, cakes, and breads, and with ice cream. Next time you have a barbecue, try grilling banana for dessert. You can grill the whole fruit with the peel slit along the top; it will be especially delicious if basted with coconut milk or honey. Banana is also a popular addition to sandwich spreads. One favorite spread calls for a mixture of chopped chicken, pineapple, celery, banana, and mayonnaise. Sliced banana is delicious in a

sandwich with peanut butter and raisins.

Plantain must be cooked before eating and is often served hot as a starchy vegetable rather than a dessert. The usual method is to slice the fruit and sauté it in a frying pan with butter, sugar, and lemon juice until soft. Try cooking green bananas this way too.

■ Banana varieties The many varieties of banana range from just a few feet to more than 25 feet high. Smaller, dwarf varieties are better adapted to most garden situations because of their compact size and the fact that the fruit matures faster. The variety chart on the opposite page lists the most common banana varieties with an emphasis on smaller selections bearing fruit that can be eaten fresh. Many varieties are known by different names, depending on where they are grown. The most common of these synonyms are listed after each preferred variety name.

The male banana flower develops at the end of the fruit stalk.

Bananas mature on a fruiting stalk that can weigh up to 100 pounds.

Bagging green bananas with an apple hastens ripening.

BANANA VARIETIES

Variety	Height (in feet)	Comments
'AeAe'	10–14	Multicolored white and green fruit can be cooked or eaten fresh when fully ripe. Green and white variegated foliage may revert to solid color, depending on soil pH.
'Apple' ('Manzano', 'Go Sai Heong')	10–15	Fingers 4–5" long with thin, yellow skin; 6–7 hands per 25–45 lb. bunch. Flesh dry but has good flavor and an apple aroma. Astringent if not fully ripe.
'Chinese' ('Dwarf Cavendish', 'Dwarf Chinese')	7–10	Fingers 6–8" long with creamy yellow skin; 6–9 hands per 40–90 lb. bunch. Sweet flavor. Good for Florida. Does not store well. A shorter form of 'Cavendish', the most popular banana in the world.
'Cocos' ('Dwarf Bluefields')	10–15	Fingers 5–7" long with bright yellow skin; 8–12 hands per 60–100 lb. bunch. Excellent flavor.
'Double Mahoi'	5–7	Can produce two or more bunches from a single stem. Cold tolerant. Small, sweet fruit.
'Dwarf Brazilian' ('Santa Carina Prata')	10–15	Fingers 5–6" long with yellow skin; 5–7 hands per 25–50 lb. bunch. Mild but delicious flavor.
'Dwarf Colorado Blanco'	7	Maroon skin, orange flesh, good flavor. Attractive ornamental with red trunk and leaves.
'Dwarf Orinoco'	7	Fingers 8–12" long; 5–9 hands per 40–50 lb. bunch. Squarish, thick-skinned fruit. Best flavor when fully ripe. Dry texture, usually cooked. Good wind and cold tolerance. Also called horse banana or burro.
'Dwarf Red Jamaican'	6–8	Small, maroon skin, excellent sweet orange flesh. Dull red leaves and trunk.
'Ebun Musak'	10–12	Fingers 4–6" long, pointed, ripen green to slightly yellow. Chocolate brown trunk.
'Enano Gigante'	6–8	Large bunches of delicious rich, creamy fruit. 'Williams' type. Heavy producer. Commercially grown in Mexico and Central America. Mature leaves dark green; red markings on new growth.
'Golden Aromatic'	10–12	Fingers 6–9" long with golden yellow skin; 4–5 hands per 30–40 lb. bunch. Very good flavor. Stores well.
'Goldfinger'	10–12	Fingers 6–8" long. Easy to grow, plant resistant to disease, cold, and wind. Fruit may not develop dark yellow coloration; look for slight color change to determine when to pick.
'Grand Nain'	6–8	Fingers up to 12" long, 50–70 pounds per bunch. Attractive, wind-resistant plant. Commercial variety from Central America.
'Haa Haa'	7	Medium-size bunches, yellow skin, orange flesh, delicious. Heavy, sturdy trunk.
'Hi-Color Mini'	2	Small fruit. Great in containers or as houseplant.
'Ice Cream' ('Java Blue')	10–15	Fingers 5–6" long with bluish silver skin that turns pale yellow when ripe; 7–9 hands per 40–60 lb. bunch. Sweet flavor; texture similar to that of ice cream. Good fresh or cooked.
'Kru'	10–12	Reddish skin, orange flesh, delicious. Foliage and trunk pigmented dark red. Sturdy.
'Monthan'	14–16	Long, heavy bunches of sweet, plump fruit. Cold tolerant.
'Pitogo'	10–12	Resembles tennis ball in shape and size. Excellent flavor.
'Popoulu'	14	Plump, salmon pink fruit with delicious applelike flavor. Slender plant prefers sheltered location with filtered light.
'Rajapuri' ('Raja Puri')	7–10	Medium-size, sweet, high-quality fruit. Tolerant of wind and cold.
'Super Dwarf Cavendish' ('Novak')	3–4	Small, sweet fruit. Ideal for containers or indoors.
'Thousand Fingers'	12–14	Hundreds of small, 1½" fruits on 8–10' long clusters. Unique, conversation piece.
'Valery' ('Taiwan', 'Tall Mons Mari')	10–15	Fingers 7–10" long with yellow skin; 8–10 hands per 60–90 lb. bunch. 'Cavendish' type. Good flavor. Cold tolerant.
'Walha'	10–15	Fingers 5–7" long; 5–6 hands per 20–50 lb. bunch. Mild but delicious flavor similar to that of 'Dwarf Brazilian'. Erroneously called 'Dwarf Apple'.
'Williams' ('Giant Cavendish', 'Giant Chinese', 'Mons Mari')	6–8	Fingers 7–9" long with yellow skin and tapered tip; 9–12 hands per 60–90 lb. bunch. Good flavor. Cold tolerant and wind resistant.

Cherimoya

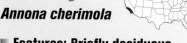

Annona cherimola

- **Features: Briefly deciduous tree; delicious fruit**
- **Size: 15–25'H×15–25'W**
- **Hardiness: 29°F**
- **Harvest: Main season February through April**

Native to mountain valleys of Peru and Ecuador, cherimoya usually elicits a two-stage response from someone experiencing it for the first time—amazement and then delight. The amazement is sparked by the unusual appearance of the fruit, which looks something like an artichoke crossed with a pineapple. Large and heartshape with green skin, it looks as if it's made of overlapping scales. The delight is a reaction to the flavor of the fruit. Cherimoya has a wonderful custardy texture and delicious tropical flavor with overtones of pineapple, banana, and papaya. Mark Twain described the flavor as "deliciousness itself."

An attractive tree that is briefly deciduous in spring, cherimoya bears big leaves about 10 inches long by 4 inches wide. They are dull green on top and velvety green on the bottom. Cherimoya usually is grown as a spreading, single-trunk tree 12 to 15 feet tall. Cherimoya grows rapidly when young, but growth slows as the tree ages.

Cherimoyas have white flesh with a delicious flavor, custardlike texture, and large black seeds.

Adaptation Cherimoya grows best in areas where summers are moderately warm with low relative humidity and where winter temperatures drop below 45°F but seldom below freezing. Optimum summer temperatures range between 70° and 85°F, but the trees will produce in warmer areas. Winters should provide some chilling but be relatively frost free, because the fruit hangs on the tree through the cold months and will be damaged by freezing temperatures. The tree tolerates brief periods of temperatures as low as 29°F. Prolonged exposure to subfreezing temperatures causes serious dieback. When cherimoya does not receive enough chilling, the tree slowly goes dormant and then experiences delayed releafing. It needs between 50 and 100 hours of temperatures between 32° and 45°F.

Southern California provides the best conditions for growing cherimoya in the United States. The largest commercial plantings

Collect pollen from flowers in the male phase (petals will be wide open). This phase normally develops in the afternoon.

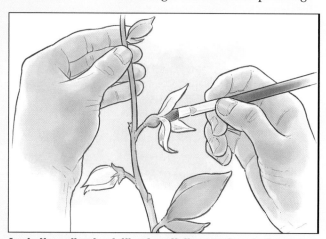

Apply the pollen to pistils of partially open female flowers.

Cherimoya is a small to medium tree with coarse-textured, dense foliage.

Watering The tree needs plenty of moisture while it is growing actively but should be watered sparingly when it is dormant. Cherimoya is susceptible to root rot in soggy soils, especially in cool weather. A drought-stressed tree will drop its leaves, exposing the fruit to sunburn.

Fertilizing Feed cherimoya on a regular basis. Apply about 2 ounces of a balanced fertilizer, such as 8-8-8, to young trees each month during the growing season until mid- or late summer. Increase the applications by an ounce each year until the tree begins to bear fruit. A mature tree should receive a pound of 8-8-8 fertilizer per inch of trunk diameter (measured at chest level). A tree may also benefit from foliar applications of micronutrients.

Pruning Cherimoya has rather brittle wood. Prune during the dormant period to develop strong branches that can support the heavy fruit. When pruning select branches with a wide angle of attachment. These branches are more strongly attached than those with narrow angles. Cherimoya fruits on new growth that originates from one-year-old wood. Prune to encourage new

are located slightly inland from the Pacific Ocean near Santa Barbara. Some varieties perform better in coastal or inland areas; these are noted on the variety chart on page 77. Cherimoya does not adapt well to the tropical lowlands of Florida and Hawaii; the atemoya (see "Cherimoya relatives" on page 76) is a better choice in those locations.

Pollination The cherimoya flower is perfect, meaning it contains both male and female parts, but self-pollination usually doesn't take place because the stigma (the female flower part) usually is receptive only on the day before pollen is released. In areas where the plant is native, a species of insect spreads the pollen at the appropriate times. This insect isn't found in the United States, which means you will have to pollinate the flowers by hand to ensure fruit production. The plants flower over a long period in midsummer, so if you pollinate every couple of days during bloom, the harvest period will extend over several months the following winter and spring.

Sometimes the flowers self-pollinate when warm weather causes the pollen to mature early or when high humidity prolongs the receptiveness of the stigma. For this reason trees in the coastal areas of California set more self-pollinated fruit than those in the drier interior valleys. Some gardeners in drier parts of the Southwest use fogging systems to raise the humidity around the blooming trees; this increases self-pollination, but it is usually better to pollinate the flowers yourself if you want well-formed fruit. Self-pollinated fruits tend to be misshapen because not all the seeds develop.

Some selected varieties seem to have a higher percentage of self-pollination, but their performance varies from area to area.

Site selection and planting The tree prefers full sun and a deep, well-drained soil with a pH between 6 and 7. If drainage is poor, plant on raised mounds.

Cherimoya in the landscape Use cherimoya as a specimen, background tree, or screen. Its size prevents it from being grown in all but the largest containers.

Nearly ripe 'White' cherimoya

Cherimoya (continued)

'El Bumpo' cherimoya has knobby skin.

Cherimoya (top) has larger leaves and whiter flowers with shorter stems compared to atemoya (bottom).

growth and fruiting near the center of the tree, where the fruit will be protected from sunburn and birds. Also a heavy crop at the outside of the tree can bend branches to the ground, causing the fruit to become dirty and bruised. Cherimoya is often pruned severely to reduce the size of the tree and ease hand pollination. Some growers prune trees to develop a trunk only 24 to 30 inches tall. Delayed flowering and fewer flowers often result, but hand pollination is easier to do.

▓ **Pests and diseases** Under good growing conditions cherimoya has few serious troubles, though nematodes can be a problem in older trees, and scales, whiteflies, and mealybugs are occasional problems on trees of any age.

▓ **Harvest and storage** Cherimoya develops a pale green to creamy yellow-green color as it reaches maturity. It should be picked when still firm and allowed to soften at room temperature. Ripe fruit yields to soft pressure. Overripe fruit is dark brown. Fruit left on the tree too long usually cracks or splits and begins to

decay. You'll probably have to harvest fruit every couple of days if you pollinated over an extended period. The fruit should be clipped, rather than pulled, from the tree. Cut the stem close to the fruit so it won't puncture other fruit during storage.

Store mature fruit above 55°F to prevent chilling injury to the skin and flesh. Ripe fruit quickly deteriorates but can be stored at temperatures lower than 55°F for short periods, although it may discolor.

▓ **Cherimoya relatives** Many close relatives of cherimoya also bear delicious fruit.

Sweetsop or sugar apple (*Annona squamosa*) is similar to cherimoya but is better adapted to Florida. The fruit is noticeably knobbier and has a sweeter flavor and less creamy texture. The tree is slightly smaller, rarely exceeding 15 feet high. Sweetsop is not hardy below 29°F. The plant is usually grown from seed.

Atemoya, a hybrid of cherimoya and sweetsop, combines the hardiness of cherimoya—mature trees are hardy to about 24° to 26°F—with sweetsop's tolerance of warm, humid climates. It is most widely planted in Florida. You can choose from many

varieties, some of which are still being evaluated. 'Gefner' reliably produces good fruit without hand pollination. 'African Pride' requires hand pollination for large crops. The flavor of atemoya's fruit is delicious, but it has a fibrous texture. For that reason it is often juiced rather than eaten out of hand. Atemoya's tree habit and cultural requirements are similar to those of cherimoya.

Another cherimoya relative, soursop (*Annona muricata*), has fruit covered with long, curved, fleshy spines. The tree is upright and may reach 20 feet high and 15 feet wide. Less hardy than sweetsop, soursop usually is damaged when the temperature drops below 30°F. Seedling-grown trees are not reliable producers of quality fruit. The most readily available selected soursop variety is called 'Fiberless Cuban'. It must be vegetatively propagated.

▓ **Cherimoya at the table** The fruit is best served chilled, cut in half or quartered, and eaten with a spoon. Adding anything to the fruit is likely to mask its wonderful fragrance and encumber its delicious tropical flavor. The fruit can also be juiced or used to make delicious sorbets or milkshakes. Ripe cherimoyas can be frozen and eaten like ice cream.

Sweetsop, *Annona squamosa*

Soursop, *Annona muricata*, a cherimoya relative, bears extremely large fruits with curved spines.

CHERIMOYA VARIETIES

Variety	Fruit description	Ripening season	Comments
'Bays'	Medium, skin smooth, yellow-green, very good sweet-tart flavor.	Dec–Apr	Spreading tree. Well adapted to coastal California.
'Booth'	Small to medium, cone shape, skin slightly knobby, yellowish green, many seeds, papaya flavor.	Nov–Mar	California heirloom. Partially self-pollinating in coastal areas. Cold tolerant.
'Chaffey'	Small to medium, thick smooth skin resists bruises, rich lemon flavor.	Jan–Apr	Vigorous, open habit, somewhat weak limbed. Hardy.
'El Bumpo'	Medium, soft skin, very knobby, excellent flavor.	Dec–Mar	California introduction.
'Fin de Jete' ('Jete')	Medium to large, juicy, sweet, black specks just under skin in mature fruit.	Feb–May	Main commercial variety of Spain.
'Honeyhart'	Medium, skin smooth, plated, yellowish green, very juicy, smooth texture, excellent flavor.	Nov–Mar	California introduction.
'Ott'	Small to medium, skin thick with smooth heart-shape plates, seedy, excellent sweet pineapple-banana flavor but can be dry and gritty.	Jan–Apr	Resists bruising. Vigorous habit.
'Pierce'	Small to large, skin knobby, light green, few seeds, very sweet, pineapple-banana flavor.	Jan–Mar	Partially self-pollinating. Has tendency toward alternate bearing.
'Spain' ('MacPherson')	Small to large, cone shape, skin smooth, dark green, sweet, juicy, good banana flavor.	Dec–Apr	Vigorous, pyramidal tree, partially self-fruitful in coastal areas, fruit prone to cracking.
'White' ('Dr. White')	Large, skin rough with small bumps, sweet papaya-mango flavor.	Dec–Mar	Open, spreading tree, good along the California coast, heat tolerant but not cold hardy.

GALLERY OF SUBTROPICAL PLANTS *(continued)*

Feijoa

Pineapple guava
Acca sellowiana
(Feijoa sellowiana)

- **Features: Evergreen shrub, silvery green foliage, beautiful flowers, distinctively flavored fruit**
- **Size: 8–20'H×8–20'W**
- **Hardiness: 15°F**
- **Harvest: September through November**

Native to tropical and subtropical highlands of South America, feijoa is an attractive shrub that bears delicious fruit with an unusual and refreshing pineapple-mint flavor. The fruits vary in shape from round to an elongated pear shape. The waxy skin is dull blue-green when harvested but turns shiny green if rubbed. The fruit is best when fresh.

Adaptation Feijoa is widely adapted to areas of the West and Southeast where winter temperatures do not fall below 15°F. The highest-quality fruit is produced in areas with moderate summers (80° to 90°F) and cool winters. A small amount of winter chilling (between 100 and 200 hours) ensures an abundant bloom. Fruit production is unreliable in southernmost Florida, where fewer than 50 hours of chilling occur.

Feijoa blossom petals are edible.

Waxy-skinned feijoas

Even though feijoa is fairly hardy, sudden fall frosts can damage ripening fruit, and late-spring frosts can destroy blossoms. Spring frost damage is most likely in mild-winter areas, where the plant is not completely hardened off and responds to warm spells by blooming early. In colder areas feijoa usually doesn't flower until after the danger of frost has passed.

Propagation The seeds of feijoa germinate easily, but the seedlings grow slowly and rarely produce quality fruit. Success with cuttings, even under mist, differs among varieties. Various grafting methods are sometimes successful, as is layering.

Because plants sucker readily, grafted plants must be trained to grow with no branches below the graft union. Cutting-grown plants of named varieties are the most desirable because they can be trained in a variety of ways. Cuttings can be maintained as multitrunk shrubs without concern that suckers will develop into rogue (off-type) branches.

Site selection and planting Feijoa fruit quality declines if the temperature regularly exceeds 100°F, and the fruit can sunburn. Also when the ripe fruits fall to the ground (a sign of peak quality), they spoil rapidly at high temperatures. To protect the fruit choose a planting site away from hot, reflected sun.

Feijoa is a handsome choice for the landscape.

In desert areas plant feijoa where it will receive partial shade during the heat of the day. Most varieties are partially self-fruitful. For maximum yields of self-sterile types plant more than one variety.

Feijoa will grow in a wide variety of soils. The best harvests, however, come from plants in well-drained soil with a pH between 5.5 and 7. Although feijoa is fairly salt tolerant, salinity slows growth and reduces yields.

Feijoa in the landscape Feijoa doubles handsomely as a landscape shrub. Its leaves are soft green on top and silvery underneath, flashing nicely in a gentle breeze. In late spring the shrub is covered with inch-wide white flowers with scarlet stamens. Feijoa responds well to pruning or shearing, but wait until early summer—after you've enjoyed the flowers. When planted close together the shrubs make a good hedge, screen, or windbreak. Feijoa can also be espaliered or trained as a small tree with one or more trunks.

Caring for feijoa

Watering The thick leaves of feijoa are slow to show signs of moisture stress. They can survive considerable drought, but lack of water will cause the fruit to drop. For quality harvests water deeply on a regular basis and mulch the soil around the plant to protect the shallow roots.

Fertilizing Feijoa plants require only light applications of a complete fertilizer.

Pruning Cutting-grown plants can be developed as shrubs with single or multiple trunks. Grafted plants must have a single trunk below the graft union. See "Propagation", on page 78.

Pruning is not required to keep plants productive, but a light pruning in summer after harvest will encourage new growth and increase yields the following year. You may want to thin the plant for easier harvesting. When grown as a hedge, feijoa responds well to heavy pruning or shearing, but it will produce fewer flowers and fruits if the pruning occurs close to bloom.

Pests and diseases Feijoa rarely develops any serious disease or insect problems.

Harvest and storage As the fruits mature, their color changes almost imperceptibly. The best way to tell when a fruit is fully ripe is to allow it to fall from the tree. Giving the tree a shake every couple of days and gathering the fallen fruits from the ground is the usual method of harvesting. To keep the fruits from bruising, place a tarp or other large cloth under the tree to catch them as they fall. This will also help keep the fruit clean and free of the soil organisms that promote spoilage. Fruit can also be picked when firm and mature and allowed to ripen at room temperature.

Mature fruit can be stored in the refrigerator for about a week, but after that the quality declines rapidly. To prevent peeled fruit from discoloring, dip it in a water–lemon juice mixture immediately after peeling.

Feijoa at the table Most people simply cut the fruit in half and scoop out the sweet flesh with a spoon. The seeds are small and edible. Feijoa is high in acid and pectin and makes excellent jellies and preserves. Fresh fruit can be quartered and eaten out of hand, or sliced and used as a garnish.

Feijoa tastes like a cross between mint and pineapple.

Sliced feijoa also adds a new dimension to fresh fruit compote. The edible white flower petals enhance salads and ice cream or provide a lovely garnish. If you pluck the petals carefully from the shrub, the flowers will continue to develop into fruit.

FEIJOA VARIETIES

Variety	Fruit description	Comments
'Choiceana'	Small to medium, midseason, oblong, fair to good quality.	Self-sterile, must be cross-pollinated.
'Coolidge'	Small to medium, late, pear-shape, fair to good quality.	Self-fertile, productive, variable fruit size, excellent garden variety.
'Edenvale' ('Improved Coolidge')	Large, late, oblong, quality very good to excellent.	Self-fertile, productive, grows slowly, good in coastal conditions.
'Edenvale Late'	Medium, late, oblong, quality very good to excellent.	Self-fertile, very productive, grows slowly, good in coastal conditions.
'Edenvale Supreme'	Medium, late, oblong, quality very good to excellent.	Self-fertile, productive, grows slowly, best eaten soon after harvest, good in coastal conditions.
'Mammoth'	Medium to large, midseason to late, round to oval, good quality, thick skin, gritty flesh.	Self-fertile but bears larger fruit with cross-pollination; vigorous plant.
'Nazemetz'	Large, late, pear-shape, thin skin, sweet pulp, excellent quality.	Self-fertile, one of the best garden varieties.
'Pineapple Gem'	Small, late, round, very good quality.	Bears heavier yields if cross-pollinated, poor in cool coastal conditions.
'Superba'	Small to medium, late, round, fair to good quality.	Self-sterile, must be cross-pollinated.
'Trask'	Medium, midseason, round, thick skin, gritty flesh, fair to good quality.	Partially self-fertile, produces more fruit if cross-pollinated, vigorous plant.
'Triumph'	Small, midseason, pear-shape, thick skin, gritty flesh, good to very good quality.	Bears heavier yields if cross-pollinated, vigorous plant.

Fig

Ficus carica

- **Features: Deciduous tree, bold branching pattern, delicious fruit**
- **Size: 15–50'H×20–60'W**
- **Hardiness: 12°–15°F**
- **Harvest: Often two crops, one in late spring, another in fall**

A fig tree has a dramatic presence wherever it is grown. Native to the eastern Mediterranean and southwestern Asia, it has silvery gray branches that are muscular and twisting, spreading wider than they are tall. The leaves are unusually large (4 to 10 inches long) and bright green, with three to five rounded lobes. In winter the tree provides a strong silhouette against cloudy skies; in summer its foliage lends a beautiful tropical feeling.

Besides high marks for beauty, fig is relatively easy to grow and remarkably adaptable. It is productive with or without heavy pruning. Even if the plant is frozen to the ground in the winter, it can spring back and bear fruit the following summer. In a container fig is an eyecatching specimen indoors or outdoors.

Though the fig is commonly

Figs come in many shapes, sizes, and colors.

called a fruit, it is really a cluster of inside-out, fleshy flowers. Each flower can develop into a seed if pollinated. The fruit may seem to contain slightly crunchy seeds, but these are actually undeveloped seedless fruitlets that are not viable.

There are basically four types of fig: the common fig, Caprifig, Smyrna fig, and San Pedro fig. Only varieties of the common fig will set two crops of fruit without pollination. The first crop is borne in spring on the previous season's growth and is called the breba crop. The second crop, borne in fall on the new growth, is known as the main crop. In cold climates spring frosts often destroy the

breba crop. Pruning also limits that crop.

Caprifigs and Smyrna figs are rarely offered to home gardeners because pollination from a specific type of wasp is necessary for fruit production. These wasps are usually not found in North America. San Pedro figs produce a breba crop without pollination and will grow in cool-summer climates.

Adaptation Fig is generally best adapted to areas with long, hot summers. Fig adapts well to hot, dry climates and will survive periods of drought, although fruit quality is much better with regular irrigation. Most commercial fig plantations are found in the warm interior valleys of California. Some fig varieties, however, require less heat to ripen their fruit and can be grown in cooler climates with short summers. In such areas figs are often shrubs, having frozen to the ground in winter. Mulching and wise site selection are important to successful fig culture in colder climates.

When fully dormant a fig tree can withstand temperatures of 12° to 15°F. In late spring and early fall, the tree is more sensitive and can be damaged at higher temperatures. Because

Large lobed leaves and twisting branches make figs prized landscape trees.

Fig is an attractive container plant.

Yellow-skinned 'Alma' fig

Breba figs are borne on the previous year's growth. This variety is 'Genoa'.

'Brown Turkey' fig

of its low chilling requirement, trees sometimes break dormancy during warm spells in winter or early spring, only to be damaged when cold weather returns.

In the Southeast, where the dried fruit beetle is a serious pest, gardeners are limited to growing varieties that have fruit with a closed eye. The eye is the small hole in the plump end of a fig through which the flowers are pollinated by a wasp in the tree's native habitat. If the dried fruit beetle enters the eye, the fruit is usually ruined. Fruit flies and various fruit rots are problems with large-eye varieties grown in the Southeast and can be troublesome in the West.

■ **Propagation** Figs propagate easily from dormant hardwood cuttings. Select one-year-old, fully mature shoots, ³⁄₈ to ⁵⁄₈ inch in diameter and 8 to 12 inches long. Bury them upright in the soil, leaving one node exposed. If freezing weather is expected, cover the whips completely or bring them indoors for protection. By spring the ends of the cuttings should have a soft white callus growth. Transplanted or left in place, the new plants should be well rooted and established by the end of summer.

■ **Site selection and planting** Choose a planting site with full sun and well-drained soil. Figs tolerate a variety of soils except salty or alkaline ones. In areas with short (less than 120 days between frosts), cool summers, espalier a tree against a south-facing, light-colored wall to take advantage of the reflected heat. The shallow, aggressive roots of fig can damage sidewalks, paving, and foundations. Allow plenty of room for them to spread.

■ **Fig in the landscape** With large, dramatic foliage and muscular branching, fig is an exceptional landscape tree. It can be used as a specimen or shade tree, and it grows well in containers. Since a tree is amenable to pruning, it can be grown against a wall as an espalier or confined to small spaces in the garden.

■ **Caring for fig trees** Established fig trees can survive with a minimum of watering, fertilizing, and pruning. For a top-quality harvest, however, provide these simple care routines.

■ **Watering** In all climates water a young fig tree regularly until it is fully established. In dry western climates water a mature tree deeply at least every one or two weeks; desert gardeners may have to water more frequently. Southern gardeners may need to water only in dry spells. Mulch the soil around the tree to conserve moisture. If a tree is not getting enough water, the leaves will turn yellow and drop. Also drought-stressed trees are more susceptible to nematode damage.

WIDELY ADAPTED FIG VARIETIES

Variety	Fruit description	Comments
'Brown Turkey' ('California Large Black', 'San Piero', 'San Piero Black')	Medium, skin is purplish brown, flesh pinkish amber. Good flavor, best when fresh.	Light breba crop. Small, hardy, vigorous tree. Prune severely for heaviest main crop.
'Celeste' ('Blue Celeste', 'Celestial', 'Honey', 'Malta', 'Sugar', 'Violette')	Small to medium, skin light violet to violet-brown, flesh reddish amber, tightly closed eye. Very sweet, usually dried.	Light breba crop. Small, productive, hardy.
'Texas Everbearing' ('Eastern Brown Turkey', 'Everbearing')	Medium to large, skin thick and mahogany-purple, flesh strawberry. Best fresh.	Light breba crop. Can be grown in the Southwest and Southeast. Vigorous but spreading. Prune to force new growth.

Fig *(continued)*

■ **Fertilizing** Recommendations for feeding a fig tree vary depending on where you live. Avoid overfertilizing. Too much nitrogen causes excess foliage growth at the expense of fruit production, and the fruit that is produced often ripens improperly if at all.

As a general rule fertilize a fig tree if the branches grew less than a foot during the previous year. Apply ½ to 1 pound of actual nitrogen, divided into three or four applications beginning in late winter or early spring and ending in July. Use the same timetable for younger trees, but use a balanced fertilizer according to the instructions on the fertilizer label.

■ **Pruning** Prune a young fig tree to establish a strong framework. After that prune occasionally to remove deadwood and to prevent the tree from becoming overgrown. Thin once in a while to keep the inner branches productive.

Even though it can get along without it, a mature fig tree responds well to pruning. You can espalier the tree or prune heavily for size control without sacrificing the main crop if you prune when the tree is dormant. Although dormant-season pruning can increase the main crop, it removes flower buds and thus reduces or eliminates the breba crop.

■ **Pests and diseases** Aside from fruit flies and beetles, which infest fruit with open eyes (see "Adaptation" on page 80), fig trees have few diseases or pests.

■ **Harvest and storage** Allow figs to fully ripen on the tree before picking them. Figs that are picked when immature will not ripen. A ripe fruit is slightly soft and starts to bend at the neck. Harvest the fruit gently to avoid bruising it.

Some people are sensitive to the foliage and milky white sap of the fig tree. If you have sensitive skin, wear a long-sleeve shirt and gloves while harvesting.

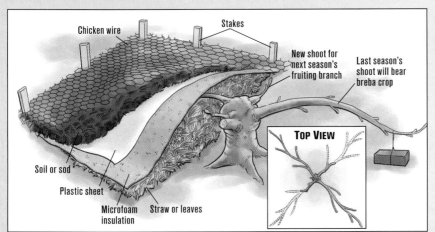

In cold climates train figs with two fruiting branches low on the trunk. During the growing season select shoots growing at a 90-degree angle to the limbs currently bearing fruit. These will bear next year's breba crop. Cover the plant in the fall.

FIG VARIETIES GROWN PRIMARILY IN THE SOUTHEAST

Variety	Fruit description	Comments
'Alma'	Medium, skin light yellow, flesh amber-tan, small eye, very sweet. Good fresh or dried.	Light breba crop, heavy main crop. Requires long, warm summers. Hardy, small tree.
'Excell'	Large, skin yellow, flesh light amber, small eye, very sweet. Excellent all-purpose fig.	Light breba crop. Fruits similar in size to 'Kadota' but more productive. Vigorous tree.
'Green Ischia' ('Verte')	Small, skin greenish yellow, flesh strawberry. Excellent fresh or dried.	Good breba crop. Recommended for short-summer climates. Small tree.
'Jelly'	Medium, long-necked, skin yellow, flesh clear apple green. Amost seedless.	Vigorous, spreading canopy.
'LSU Everbearing'	Small, skin light yellow, flesh white to yellow. Very sweet.	Vigorous. Large crop, ripens July to frost.
'LSU Gold'	Medium, skin light yellow, flesh yellow. Very sweet.	Resists splitting. Vigorous, productive.
'LSU Improved Celeste'	Medium to large, skin light brown to violet, strawberry pink flesh, tight eye. Excellent dried.	Resists rot. Hardy.
'LSU Purple'	Small to medium, skin purple, flesh light yellow to red. Fine flavor.	Vigorous tree.
'Magnolia' ('Brunswick', 'Madonna')	Medium, skin reddish brown, flesh strawberry, rich flavor. Does not dry well.	Light breba crop. Develops best flavor and size with caprification (pollination by hanging branches with male flowers of Caprifig in tree). Vigorous, hardy tree.

Fresh figs do not keep well; they can be stored in the refrigerator for only two to three days.

Some fig varieties are delicious when dried. In hot and dry climates, collect figs that are to be dried as they drop from the tree. In humid or wet climates, pick the fruits as ripe as possible but before they fall. Before drying the figs, peel and quarter them. Figs take four to five days to dry in the sun and 10 to 12 hours in a dehydrator. When dry the fruit should be pliable and slightly sticky but not wet. Dried figs can be stored for six to eight months.

▮ **Figs at the table** Fig lovers usually prefer fresh figs. Serve them peeled and quartered on a bed of dressed bitter greens such as arugula (this is particularly attractive with the 'Black Mission' fig), wrapped in prosciutto and secured with a toothpick, or accompanied by Gorgonzola cheese for dessert.

'Mission' fig

FIG VARIETIES GROWN PRIMARILY IN THE WEST

Variety	Fruit description	Comments
'Adriatic' ('Strawberry Fig', 'Verdone', 'White Adriatic')	Small to medium, skin greenish, flesh strawberry. Good all-purpose fig.	Light breba crop. Large, vigorous tree leafs out early, subject to frost damage. Prune to force new growth.
'Black Jack'	Large, skin purplish, flesh pink. Very sweet.	Small tree, good for pots or smaller gardens.
'Black Mission' ('California Large Black', 'Franciscan', 'Mission')	Large, skin purplish black, flesh pink. Excellent, all-purpose fig.	Good breba crop of large fruit. Large vigorous tree produces best when not heavily pruned. Main California commercial variety.
'Conadria'	Medium, skin greenish yellow to white with purplish blush, flesh strawberry, mildly sweet. Good fresh, excellent dried.	Early breba crop. Vigorous tree, best in hot climates.
'Flanders'	Medium, long-necked, skin brownish yellow with violet stripes, flesh amber, strong, fine flavor. Excellent, all-purpose fruit.	Good breba crop. Ripens late.
'Genoa' ('White Genoa')	Medium, skin greenish yellow to white, flesh yellow-amber, sweet. Good fresh or dried.	Light breba and main crops. Fruit has large eye and hollow center. Best adapted to cooler regions.
'Italian Honey' ('Blanche', 'Lattarula', 'Lemon', 'White Marseille')	Medium to large, skin yellowish green, flesh white to amber, sweet, lemon flavor.	Light breba crop. Good in short-season, cool-summer areas. Slow-growing, dense, hardy tree.
'Kadota' ('Dottato', 'Florentine', 'White Kadota')	Medium, skin yellowish green, flesh amber, rich flavor. Excellent all-purpose fig.	Little or no breba crop. Requires hot, dry climate for best quality. Vigorous tree.
'King' ('Desert King')	Large, skin dark green, flesh purple, sweet. Delicious fresh or dried.	Good breba crop, no main crop. Hardy, well adapted to cool areas such as the Pacific Northwest. Do not prune severely.
'Osborne Prolific' ('Archipel', 'Neveralla')	Medium to large, skin dark reddish brown, flesh amber, very sweet. Best fresh.	Light breba crop. Hardy. Reliable in areas with cool, short summers, such as coastal California.
'Panachee' ('Striped Tiger', 'Tiger Fig')	Small to medium, skin greenish yellow with dark green stripes, flesh strawberry, dry but sweet. Best fresh.	No breba crop. Unusual-looking fig. Requires long, warm growing season. Ripens late. Medium eye.
'Pasquale' ('Verino')	Small, skin dark purplish black, flesh dark strawberry, fine flavor, very sweet. Excellent fresh or dried.	Good breba crop. Main crop ripens very late, susceptible to fall frost damage.
'Peter's Honey'	Medium, skin greenish yellow, dark amber flesh, great flavor. Excellent fresh.	Productive.
'Tena'	Small, skin light green, flesh amber, fine flavor. Good fresh or dried.	Good breba crop. Bears heavily. Medium eye.

Guava
Psidium spp.

- **Features:** Evergreen shrub or small tree, fragrant flowers, delicious fruit
- **Size:** 10–25'H×8–25'W
- **Hardiness:** Tropical guava 29°F, strawberry guava 24°F
- **Harvest:** Spring to fall, some ripen year-round

Two common types of guavas grown in the United States are tropical guava *(Psidium guajava)* and strawberry guava *(P. littorale,* also sometimes called *P. cattleianum),* both of which are native to tropical Central and South America. Strawberry guava comes in two forms: One is the red-fruited, *P. littorale longipes,* and the other is the yellow-fruited *P. littorale littorale,* more commonly referred to as lemon guava. Both kinds of guava are attractive evergreen plants with shedding bark and fragrant flowers, but they differ in size, fruit quality, and adaptation.

Lemon guava turns yellow as it nears maturity.

Tropical guava bears egg-shape fruit ranging from ¼ to 3 pounds. In Southern California the fruit ripens from fall to early spring, depending on variety. The fruit is borne on attractive shrubs or small trees that can reach 20 to 25 feet high. Although usually evergreen, the deeply veined leaves may drop for a brief period in spring.

Strawberry guava is a smaller, extremely handsome plant rarely exceeding 10 to 15 feet high. Because of its beauty, it is often used as an ornamental. The glossy, deep green leaves form a perfect backdrop for the brightly colored fruit, which is preceded, and often accompanied, by lightly fragrant white flowers. The fruits are smaller than those of the tropical guava, generally 1 to 2 inches in diameter. In Southern California fruits ripen from fall through early summer. Unfortunately, there are no selected varieties and seedlings vary in quality, but the fruit of the yellow form is usually larger and sweeter. It's best to propagate plants that you know will produce sweet fruit.

- **Adaptation** Tropical guava is best adapted to the warm, humid

Red strawberry guava shines among attractive evergreen leaves.

climates of Florida and Hawaii, although it also grows well in coastal Southern California and South Texas. As its name suggests, tropical guava is sensitive to frost; a tree will recover from brief exposure to 26°F but may be completely defoliated. Strawberry guava is a much hardier plant, able to withstand brief periods of temperatures as low as 24°F. It is adapted to coastal California but does poorly in hot desert or interior areas. In South Florida and Hawaii, guavas self-seed readily and have become troublesome weeds; check with your local cooperative extension office before planting.

■ **Pollination** Guavas are primarily self-fruitful, although most produce more fruit when cross-pollinated with another variety. Plants can bloom throughout the year in tropical areas, but the heaviest bloom occurs with the onset of warm weather in spring. The exact time can vary from year to year depending on the weather. Because guavas produce flowers on the current season's growth, you can prune to stimulate bloom.

■ **Propagation** Trees are propagated by budding, grafting, or air layering. Plants can also be grown from cuttings or suckers (shoots that develop near the base of the plant). Seedlings may not produce quality fruit.

■ **Site selection and planting** Both types of guava prefer full sun and well-drained soil in the pH range of 5 to 7. They tolerate a variety of soils but produce better in rich soils high in organic matter. Tropical guava does not tolerate saline (salty) soils. Choose container-grown nursery plants carefully. A plant that is pot

Flower and immature fruits of strawberry guava with glossy green foliage

bound usually performs poorly after transplanting.

■ **Guavas in the landscape** Guavas are attractive plants that can be grown as hedges, screens, or specimens or worked into shrub borders. They also adapt well to growing in containers.

■ **Caring for guava** In areas where they are well adapted, guavas are among the easiest subtropical plants to grow.

■ **Watering** Tropical guava is most productive with regular, deep watering. Lack of moisture delays bloom and causes the fruit to drop. Strawberry guava

can withstand brief periods of drought.

■ **Fertilizing** Because tropical guava is a fast grower and heavy feeder, it benefits from regular applications of fertilizer. A mature tree may require as much as 1 pound of actual nitrogen per year applied monthly just prior to heavy pruning. Strawberry guava is less vigorous and gets by with about half as much nitrogen.

Both types may require chelated micronutrient foliar sprays when they are grown in containers or in areas with soil that is alkaline or deficient in micronutrients.

TROPICAL GUAVA JUICE VARIETIES

Variety	Fruit description	Comments
'Beaumont'	Medium, pink flesh, moderately seedy, mildly acidic flavor.	Originated in Hawaii.
'Ka Hua Kula'	Medium, flesh thick and pink, few seeds, mildly acidic flavor.	Originated in Hawaii.

Guava *(continued)*

Guava flowers are lightly fragrant.

Tropical guavas such as 'Indonesian Seedless' grow best in frost-free areas of Florida and Hawaii.

■ Pruning Both tropical and strawberry guavas respond well to pruning and can be used as informal hedges or screens. You can easily maintain a guava at 6 to 8 feet high with annual pruning.

■ Pests and diseases Foliar diseases such as anthracnose can be a problem in humid climates. Control them with regular fungicide applications. Where they are present, root-knot nematodes reduce plant vigor. Guava whitefly, guava moth, and Caribbean fruit fly can be major problems in South Florida. Whiteflies and scale insects are potential pests in California. Contact your local cooperative extension service for control measures.

■ Harvest and storage In warmer regions guavas ripen all year. There is a distinctive change in the color and aroma of a guava that has ripened. Pick pink or red guavas that will be eaten fresh when they turn from green to yellow, then allow them to soften at room temperature. Place the fruit in a brown paper bag with a banana or apple to hasten ripening. Harvest white guava when it reaches full size and the skin is green. Eat the fruit of most white-flesh varieties while it is still crunchy, before it softens and turns yellow. Some varieties are also good when the flesh turns soft and yellow.

Mature green fruits can be stored for two to five weeks at temperatures between 46° and 50°F and relative humidity of 85 to 95 percent. Fruits that have changed color cannot be stored for extended periods because they bruise easily and quickly deteriorate or rot.

■ **Guava at the table** Both kinds of guava have an exceptionally high vitamin content. They are rich in pectin and are commonly used in jellies and preserves. The fruits can also be eaten out of hand, juiced, or combined with other fruits such as banana and pineapple. Tropical guava varieties differ in seediness and in pulp color. Eat pink-pulp types when they are soft. They may be sweet and mild or stong and pungent. Use white-pulp types when they are hard and crunchy, with a sweet and sour flavor. The sweeter varieties with soft seeds are excellent eaten fresh, and all make delicious jams, jellies, preserves, and juices.

Tropical guavas have a musky, sweet flesh that can be eaten fresh or used to make juice, jams, and jellies.

TROPICAL GUAVA DESSERT VARIETIES

Variety	Fruit description	Comments
'Detwiler'	Medium to large, yellow flesh, sweet, pleasant flavor.	Originated in California.
'Hong Kong Pink'	Medium to large, flesh thick and pink, few seeds, sweet, pleasant flavor.	Originated in Hawaii.
'Indonesian Seedless'	Small to medium, flesh hard and white, usually seedless, good flavor.	Originated in Florida.
'Mexican Cream'	Small, flesh thick and white, soft seeds in small cavity, sweet and spicy.	Originated in Mexico.
'Patillo'	Small, deep-pink flesh, small seeds, mildly acidic flavor.	Originated in Florida.
'Red Indian'	Small to medium, flesh thick and red, few seeds, sprightly flavor, minimal muskiness, excellent quality.	Originated in Florida.
'Red Malaysian' ('Thai Maroon')	Medium, skin deep red, flesh reddish pink.	Originated in Asia.
'Ruby × Supreme'	Medium, flesh pinkish orange, sweet, pleasant flavor, high quality.	Originated in Florida.
'Supreme'	Large, flesh thick and white, sweet, good quality.	Originated in Florida.
'Turnbull'	Medium to large, flesh white, moderately seedy, excellent flavor. Tends to rot at flower end.	Originated in Florida.
'White Indian'	Small to medium, flesh thick and white, moderately seedy, excellent sprightly flavor.	Originated in Florida.

Kiwifruit

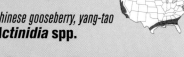

Chinese gooseberry, yang-tao
Actinidia spp.

- **Features:** Vigorous deciduous vine, attractive foliage and flowers, great-tasting fruit
- **Size:** 18–24'H×10–15'W
- **Hardiness:** 10°F
- **Harvest:** October and November

Native to eastern Asia, kiwifruit is relatively new to America. The first large commercial kiwi farms in the United States were planted about 1970. Since then this egg-shape, fuzzy-skinned fruit with shimmering emerald green flesh (*A. deliciosa*) and a delicious berry flavor has found a permanent home here. Even more recently golden kiwifruit (*A. chinensis*) with yellow or red flesh is being imported from New Zealand and China. Yellow varieties are also being planted commercially in California, but plants are not yet widely available to home gardeners.

The kiwi vine has worked its way into many American gardens. The vine is adaptable to a variety of climates, and close relatives with similar fruit (see page 91) are extremely hardy, extending kiwifruit culture into cold northern regions. In addition to

Kiwifruit plants are sprawling vines that need a strong support.

Kiwifruits have green or yellow flesh.

bearing delicious fruit, a kiwi vine has attractive foliage and flowers and an interesting twining habit.

The fruits are borne on fast-growing deciduous vines that need heavy annual pruning to keep them productive and within bounds. It is not unusual for a healthy vine to cover an area 10 to 15 feet wide, 18 to 24 feet long, and 9 to 12 feet high. The dark green leaves are round, 5 to 8 inches wide, and fuzzy white on the underside. New growth is velvety brown. The yellowish white flowers, which are about an inch in diameter, develop in the leaf joints of the new shoots. The round to oblong fruits have

This kiwifruit vine is trained to an arbor to shade a patio.

Kiwifruit vines bear attractive fuzzy leaves and creamy white flowers.

a fuzzy brown skin enclosing soft, bright green or yellow flesh dotted with tiny edible black seeds.

In commercial orchards kiwi vines are usually trained on wire trellises elevated 6 to 7 feet off the ground. In the home garden many more options are available (see "Kiwifruit in the landscape" on page 89).

Adaptation Kiwi vines can be grown in most areas of the United States where the temperature does not drop below 10°F. The flowers are susceptible to damage from late-spring frosts, and the fruit, which requires a growing season of at least 240 frost-free days to become sweet, can be damaged by hard frosts in fall. Protect the vine from strong winds; spring gusts can snap off new growth where it emerges from the canes. Kiwi vines fruit poorly in most of South Florida and are not recommended for hot desert climates.

Most kiwi varieties have chilling requirements ranging from 400 to 800 hours, but low-chill varieties such as 'Vincent' can be grown in areas with fewer than 100 hours of chilling. In mild-winter areas the vines may retain their leaves all winter and fail to flower the following spring.

Pollination The vines are either male or female; you need at least one of each for fruit production. Commercial growers plant one male surrounded by eight females with about 15 to 18 feet between plants, but a pair of vines usually supply enough fruit for home gardeners. Don't prune the male vine until early summer, after the canes have flowered and the fruit has set on the female vine. It's important to select male and female plants that have the same chilling requirements so they break dormancy and flower together. Insects are largely responsible for pollination.

▉ Propagation A kiwi vine can be propagated under mist from dormant hardwood cuttings or semihardwood cuttings taken in July or August. Many nurseries also graft selected varieties onto seedling rootstocks in May or June. In mild-winter areas there is no advantage to planting cutting-grown plants instead of grafted plants, but in cold climates cutting-grown plants are superior, because if the top of the plant is killed by frost it can resprout from the roots and still be true to type.

Seedling plants have varied chilling requirements and don't bear fruit of dependable quality, so it is best to stick with grafted or cutting-grown plants. Seedlings also take much longer to produce.

▉ Site selection and planting Kiwifruit grows in full sun or partial shade. It prefers a well-drained soil that is rich in organic matter with a pH range between 5.5 and 7. Provide protection in windy areas. Kiwi does not tolerate salty soils. Plant bare-root or container stock.

Install a sturdy trellis or other support at planting time (see "Pruning" on page 90). If you are planting just two vines, do not let the male and female intertwine or pruning will be difficult. Instead plant them 12 to 15 feet apart.

▉ Kiwifruit in the landscape Kiwi vines can be trained over an arbor to shade a patio, tied to a trellis to soften a wall, or allowed to sprawl over a fence or pergola. With any of these methods, the fruit will hang from the vine in tantalizing clusters throughout the summer. However, keep in mind that kiwi is very vigorous and, when covering an arbor, will cast dense shade and need regular pruning to keep it within bounds.

SPUR-PRUNING FOR ARBORS

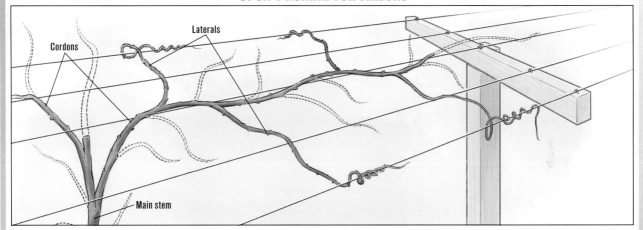

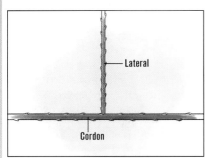

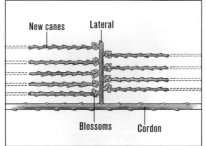

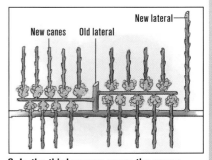

Begin training the vine by cutting back the main stem to a bud about 6 inches below the arbor (top). Train two cordons along the arbor with fruiting laterals every 24 to 30 inches. Remove all other canes.

1. During the first growing season, cut the laterals to about 4 feet. During the winter cut laterals back to 8 to 10 buds.

2. During the second growing season, after the vines flower, cut the new canes to 8 to 10 buds past the last blossom. During the winter cut the laterals to just past the cane that bore fruit the previous year.

3. In the third season prune the canes as in the second season, and allow new laterals to develop between the old ones. During winter remove any laterals that have fruited twice. Replace the fruiting laterals by cutting back other laterals to 8 to 10 buds as in Step 1.

Kiwifruit *(continued)*

▓ Caring for kiwifruit

▓ **Watering** The vigorous growth and abundant foliage of the kiwi vine call for ample soil moisture. Water deeply and frequently in a basin that extends 5 to 6 feet from the trunk. Water-stressed plants drop their leaves, exposing the fruit to sunburn. They also may not flower the following year. Keep the soil moist until harvest, but cut back on the water as fall approaches in order to encourage dormancy.

Where hot, dry winds are common in fall, mulch the ground under the entire canopy of the vine and keep it moist. This may increase the humidity enough to prevent leaf drop.

▓ **Fertilizing** Kiwi is a vigorous plant that needs about 1 pound of actual nitrogen per year. Young vines are sensitive to overfertilization; they need only one-eighth to one-quarter that amount. Spread the fertilizer evenly under the entire canopy. Late feeding may delay dormancy, so don't fertilize after midsummer. Chelated micronutrients may be needed in some areas.

▓ **Pruning** Kiwifruit vines must be pruned and trained carefully or they quickly become a fruitless, tangled mess.

There are two basic training methods: the fruiting lateral method and the spur method. The one you choose depends on how much room you have and how many plants you want to grow.

In the fruiting lateral method (preferred by most commercial growers), the vines are trained on a five-wire trellis supported 6 feet above the ground by posts topped with T-shape arms. The fruiting canes develop from permanent arms (called cordons) and are trained along the trellis wires.

The spur method is preferable where space is limited. The short fruiting spurs originate from the main trunk or permanent cordons, and the canes that grow from these spurs each season are

Clusters of nearly ripe kiwifruit weigh down this vine.

tied to a fence, wall, or trellis (see illustration on page 89).

Both training techniques require a strong support. If you build a trellis, construct it with strong materials that will last a long time. Kiwifruit can remain productive for more than 40 years. Use pressure-treated wood where the trellis will be in direct contact with the soil.

Regardless of the training method you choose, let the young plants grow with minimal pruning for a year or two after planting. If a strong main trunk, more than ¼ inch in diameter, fails to develop the first year, cut the vine back to two or three buds above the ground or graft union the following dormant season. In spring train the most vigorous shoot up the trellis. During the training period direct the plant's energy into developing a strong trunk and arms or spurs.

Prune female vines during the dormant season. Vines must be completely dormant to respond well to pruning. Some growers have successfully induced dormancy by stripping the foliage from the plants or by withholding water, but these techniques are severe and should be used only as a last resort. You will also need to prune kiwi occasionally in summer to remove vigorous shoots that are getting in the way or straying out of bounds.

Remove about half of the

'Hayward' is one of the most popular kiwifruit varieties.

growth on male vines after they have finished blooming.

▓ **Pests and diseases** Root-knot nematodes may limit yields, but kiwi vines are so vigorous and productive that you may never notice a problem. Oak root fungus infects kiwi in some California soils. Other soilborne pathogens threaten only plants in poorly drained soils. Various insects, such as leaf roller caterpillars and scale insects, can be troublesome.

The aroma of the foliage and the bark of the vine affect cats much as catnip does. They may uproot young plants or scratch the trunks of older vines.

▓ Kiwifruit varieties

▓ **Male varieties** Three varieties of male kiwi vines commonly are used as pollinators: 'Matua', 'Tomuri', and 'Chico Male'. 'Matua' is used most often because of its long blooming period. Although it usually blooms earlier than the female 'Monty' and 'Hayward' varieties, there is usually enough overlap for fruit set. The late-blooming 'Tomuri' pollinator can also be used to pollinate 'Monty' and either of the 'Hayward' varieties. 'Chico Male' is preferred by some as a pollinator for 'Chico Hayward'.

▓ **Female varieties** See the chart on the next page for descriptions of the most common varieties.

▓ **Harvest and storage** Kiwifruit usually ripens in November in hot areas, or in December in cooler

Hardy kiwi tied to an arbor

Colorful foliage of kolomikta vine

climates. Pick the fruit when it is still hard and ripen it off the vine. The trick is to know when kiwi is ready to pick. A change of color from greenish brown to brown is a sign that the fruit is almost mature. Also look for a few fruits beginning to soften on the vine. Pick the largest fruits first, giving the smaller ones a little more time to swell and sweeten. Fruits left on the vine too long will soften and decay. A light frost (31°F) will not damage the fruit and may even improve its quality, but lower temperatures will make it inedible.

Kiwifruit softens in a few days when kept at room temperature.

Unbruised mature fruits may be stored for up to six months in the refrigerator if air circulation is good and they are kept away from other ripening fruits such as apples. Check kiwifruit often while it is in storage and remove any decaying pieces.

■ **Kiwifruit relatives** Several close relatives produce delicious fruit, are very hardy, and less vigorous growers. Tara vine, or hardy kiwi (*A. arguta*), is hardy to –10°F. The plant is similar to kiwifruit, but the leaves are slightly longer and more pointed. As with kiwifruit, male and female plants usually are required for pollination. The fruit has a kiwi flavor but

is smaller—1 to 1½ inches in diameter—and can be eaten skin and all. It ripens on the vine in areas with 200 frost-free days, but it can be picked when still hard and ripened off the vine in areas with shorter growing seasons.

Hardy kiwi has attracted the attention of botanists and plant breeders around the world. Selections include self-fruitful 'Issai'. Fruiting female varieties include 'Ananasnaja' ('Anna'), 'Jumbo', 'Geneva', 'Hood River', and 'Meader #1'. Males are usually labeled simply "male." There are also hybrid forms, such as 'Ken's Red', with red fruit.

Kolomikta vine (*A. kolomikta*) is a slender, deciduous vine with variegated pink-and-white foliage and fragrant flowers. The small ½- to 1-inch fruits ripen over an extended period, making them well suited for the home garden. The plant is hardy to –40°F.

■ **Kiwifruit at the table** The fruit adds a beautiful, jewellike finishing touch to a variety of dishes when pared and sliced crosswise. It is excellent with prosciutto or coppa as an hors d'oeuvre, in salads, and as a garnish for chicken breasts. It also makes fine sorbets and jellies.

KIWIFRUIT VARIETIES

Variety	Fruit description	Comments
'Abbott'	Small unless thinned, early, round with long, soft, dense hairs. Similar to 'Allison'. Good flavor.	Vigorous, bears heavily, flowers early. Medium chilling requirement.
'Allison'	Small, larger if thinned, early, round with long, soft, dense hairs. Similar to 'Abbott'. Good flavor.	Vigorous, bears heavily, flowers early. Medium chilling requirement.
'Blake'	Small, early, oval, flavor inferior to that of 'Saanichton 12' and 'Hayward.'	Self-fruitful but produces more fruit with male close by. Low chilling requirement.
'Bruno'	Large, midseason, oblong, dark brown bristly hairs. Good flavor.	Vigorous, bears heavily, fruit must be thinned. Not for areas with short growing season. Medium chilling requirement.
'Hayward'	Large, late, oblong, pale greenish brown with fine, silky hairs. Tends to produce some odd-shape fruit.	Excellent quality. Fruit doesn't require thinning. High chilling requirement. Originated in New Zealand.
'Monty'	Small to medium, early, oblong. Good flavor.	Vigorous, bears heavily, fruit must be thinned. Flowers early. Low-quality fruit. Medium chilling requirement.
'Saanichton 12'	Large, more rectangular than 'Hayward'. Good flavor, can be a bit fibrous.	Vigorous. Discovered in British Columbia. Good in Pacific Northwest.
'Vincent'	Similar to 'Hayward' except for early ripening. Good flavor.	Vigorous, bears heavily, fruit must be thinned. Flowers and ripens early. Low chilling requirement.

Loquat

Japanese medlar,
Japanese plum
Eriobotrya japonica

- **Features: Evergreen shrub or tree, bold foliage, lightly fragrant flowers, sweet yellow fruit**
- **Size: 15–30'H×15–30'W**
- **Hardiness: Foliage to 20°F, mature tree to 10°F**
- **Harvest: January to May in Southeast, March to June in West**

Loquats are bold-textured evergreen trees that provide shade.

'Gold Nugget' loquat

Native to Japan and China, loquat is an easy-to-grow plant with boldly textured foliage and clusters of small orange-yellow fruits 1 to 2 inches in diameter. Each fruit contains three to five large seeds surrounded by sweet, tangy, aromatic flesh, which may be orange, yellow, or white.

Loquat is often grown as an ornamental tree. Its large, prominently veined leaves contrast well with plants bearing smaller, softer leaves. The leaf undersides are light green and often covered with a soft down. New growth is tinged with red.

Small, lightly fragrant white flowers bloom at the ends of branches in fall or early winter. Before they open, the flower clusters have an unusual woolly texture. In full bloom the tree is alive with bees. Most loquat varieties are self-fruitful, but cross-pollination with another variety improves fruit set and size.

Adaptation Loquat produces the best fruit in areas with mild winters and summers. Although the tree is quite hardy, 28°F will damage the flowers and ripening fruit. Prolonged heat in summer inhibits flowering. Intense heat and sunlight during winter result in sunburned fruit. White-flesh varieties are better adapted to cool coastal areas. Types with orange flesh need more warmth to produce sweet fruit.

Varieties perform differently depending on where they are grown. In the Southeast 'Bartow', 'Champagne', 'Fletcher Red', 'Hardee', 'Premier', 'SES #2', 'Thales', and 'Wolfe' are well adapted. In Florida 'Oliver' does very well; 'Advance', 'Bradenton', 'Champagne', 'Early Red', 'Pineapple', 'Premier', 'Tanaka', and 'Thales' are also grown there. In California white-flesh varieties are better adapted to cool coastal areas, and orange-flesh varieties such as 'Big Jim' and 'Gold Nugget' to warmer interior valleys. In Hawaii 'Advance' and 'Tanaka' are preferred.

Propagation Loquat varieties selected for quality fruit are usually propagated by budding or grafting. Many nurseries sell seedling-grown plants for use as ornamentals, but these trees

WHITE-FLESH LOQUAT VARIETIES

Variety	Fruit description	Comments
'Advance'	Large, midseason, oblong, yellow skin, very juicy, good quality.	Self-unfruitful. Pollinate with 'Gold Nugget'. Dwarf tree to about 5 ft. high. Resists fire blight. 'California Advance' is standard height.
'Bartow' ('Fletcher White')	Medium, midseason, pale yellow skin, good quality.	
'Benlehr'	Medium, yellow skin, juicy white flesh. Sweet, easy to peel, excellent quality.	California selection.
'Champagne'	Medium to large, late, tough, light yellow skin, good tart flavor.	Self-unfruitful. California heirloom variety.
'Hardee'	Vary large, round, midseason, pale yellow skin, fair quality.	Vigorous tree.
'MacBeth'	Medium, pale yellow skin, juicy, sweet.	Self-fertile. California introduction.
'Premier'	Large, early, oblong, pale yellow skin, very sweet.	Dwarf, slow-growing tree.

seldom produce high-quality fruit.

■ Site selection and planting Loquat grows best in full sun but also does well in partial shade. It adapts to almost any well-drained soil.

■ Loquat in the landscape A mature tree has a bold texture with a rounded canopy that can be used to shade a patio, although the heavy leaves can be messy when they drop. Loquat also makes a nice background tree, an attractive espalier, and a good container plant.

■ Caring for loquat

■ Watering Although loquat is drought tolerant, it produces much better fruit with regular, deep watering. The tree will not tolerate standing water.

■ Fertilizing Loquat benefits from regular, light applications of nitrogen fertilizer, but too much nitrogen reduces flowering. Fertilize two or three times from spring to early summer. Do not fertilize after midsummer.

■ Pruning The tree needs little pruning. To make loquat more attractive, occasionally remove crossing branches and thin any dense growth to let light into the

Golden yellow loquats ready to pick

center. The tree responds well to severe pruning and can be trained as an espalier. Prune after harvest to avoid reducing next year's crop. If fruit set is heavy, remove about half of the immature fruits when they reach ½ inch in diameter to improve the size and quality of remaining fruits.

■ Pests and diseases In Florida the Caribbean fruit fly is a serious pest. Trees may get fire blight. To control fire blight remove the scorched-looking branches, cutting well into live wood. Sterilize your shears between cuts by dipping them in a solution of household bleach diluted with

Loquat works well as an espalier.

water (1 part bleach to 9 parts water) or in undiluted rubbing alcohol. Burn the prunings or seal them in a plastic bag before disposal. Anthracnose may also infect loquat.

■ Harvest and storage Allow loquats to ripen fully before you harvest them. The fruit develops a distinctive color (white, yellow, or orange depending on the variety) and begins to soften when ripe. Ripe fruit may be stored in the refrigerator for one to two weeks.

■ Loquat at the table The fruit is delicious eaten fresh but can also be dried or used to make jams, jellies, preserves, or sauce.

YELLOW/ORANGE-FLESH LOQUAT VARIETIES

Variety	Fruit description	Comments
'Big Jim'	Large, late, oblong, pale orange skin, orange flesh, very sweet.	Self-fertile, productive. California selection. Vigorous upright tree.
'Bradenton' ('Hastings')	Large, midseason, oblong, pale yellow skin, orange flesh, excellent quality.	Vigorous upright tree.
'Early Red'	Medium to large, very early, tough orange-red skin with white dots, orange flesh, juicy, sweet-tart flavor.	California heirloom variety.
'Fletcher Red'	Large, midseason, oblong, thick orange-red skin, orange-red flesh, excellent flavor.	Slow-growing, upright tree. Fruit stores well.
'Gold Nugget'	Medium to large, round, late, deep-orange skin, yellow-orange flesh, sweet-tart apricotlike flavor.	Self-fertile. Vigorous upright tree.
'Oliver'	Large, midseason, round, deep-yellow skin, light orange flesh, excellent subacid flavor.	Vigorous tree.
'Ses 2'	Medium, midseason, oblong, pale yellow skin, yellow flesh, good flavor.	Vigorous tree. Florida selection.
'Tanaka'	Very large, late, oblong, deep-yellow skin, yellow-orange flesh, very good sweet-tart flavor.	Partially self-fruitful. Medium-size tree.
'Thales'	Medium, midseason, round, yellow skin, yellow-orange flesh, good sweet-tart flavor.	Self-fertile. Vigorous tree.
'Wolfe'	Oblong, midseason to late, pale yellow skin, white to pale yellow flesh, excellent flavor.	Florida selection. All-purpose but excellent for cooking.

Lychee

Litchi, leechee
Litchi chinensis

- **Features: Evergeen tree or large shrub, yellowish white flowers, red fruit**
- **Size: 20–40'H×20–40'W**
- **Hardiness: 25ºF**
- **Harvest: May to September**

A lychee tree in full fruit is a stunning sight. Large clusters of bright red fruit dangle among shiny, leathery, dark green leaves divided into four to eight leaflets. Lychee is also eyecatching in spring, when huge sprays of yellowish white flowers adorn it. The fruit—a translucent, sweet, gelatinous delicacy—is encased within a brittle, warty shell.

The tree has full foliage and branches to the ground. Under ideal conditions it may reach 40 feet high but is usually smaller. In most areas lychee has a tendency to bear irregularly, producing a crop every two to four years.

Ripe lychees

Bumper crop of lychees

Adaptation Lychee does best when it gets warm, humid summers for flowering and fruit development, and winter chilling for flower bud development. Most varieties need 100 to 600 hours between 32º and 45ºF. Cool winters with low amounts of rainfall are ideal.

A lychee tree becomes hardier as it ages. Mature trees survive temperatures as low as 25ºF when fully hardened; young trees may be killed by a light frost. Lychee is best adapted to the highlands of Hawaii and coastal Florida, but varieties often perform differently in each area. Lychee has also been grown successfully in relatively frost-free areas of California.

Propagation Air layering is the most common method of propagating lychee because grafting is difficult and seedlings do not reliably bear quality fruit. Grow young plants propagated by air layering in containers for one or two seasons to allow the root system to develop and increase the likelihood of successful transplanting. See page 31 for more about air layering.

Pollination Although usually self-fruitful, lychee trees produce more male than female flowers. In rare cases trees may produce only male flowers and won't set fruit.

Site selection and planting Plant in a protected location in full sun with well-drained soil that is rich in organic matter. Soil pH between 5.5 and 7.5 is acceptable, but plants grow better in soils with a pH at the low end of this range. Apply a thick layer of organic mulch to the soil after planting.

Lychee in the landscape With its striking fruit and handsome foliage, lychee makes a good specimen, background, or medium-size shade tree.

Caring for lychee

Watering Lychee requires moist (but not wet) soil, so give the tree regular water when it is growing actively. Lychee is sensitive to damage from salts in the soil or water. In the Southwest leach the soil periodically.

Fertilizing Young trees grow slowly. Give a young tree only a light application of a complete fertilizer. Mature trees are heavier feeders. Fertilize monthly from spring to summer. Avoid excess phosphorus, which can damage trees. Use a fertilizer formulated for acid-loving plants such as rhododendrons and azaleas. Chelated iron may be necessary in areas with alkaline soil.

A lychee tree in full fruiting glory bears large clusters of sweet red fruits.

Pruning Prune a young tree to establish a strong permanent structure for easy harvests. After that remove damaged or crossing branches or prune more heavily to control size.

Pests and diseases Mites, scale insects, and aphids occasionally infest lychee. Anthracnose can be a problem in Florida. Fruit splitting is caused by fluctuating soil moisture levels. Avoid this problem by watering regularly. Birds often eat both the immature and the ripe fruits; cover plants with protective netting if you find you are losing too many fruits.

Harvest and storage Allow fruits to ripen fully on the tree. Each variety has a characteristic color change as it ripens. Overly mature fruits darken, lose their luster, and lack rich flavor. Immature fruits are very acidic. Snip off entire fruit clusters, keeping a short piece of stem attached. Be careful to leave the fruit casing intact, because damaged fruits decay quickly.

Lychee begins to deteriorate within three days at room temperature. Store ripe fruits in a polyethylene bag for up to five weeks in the refrigerator. They can also be frozen or dried.

Lychee at the table Fresh lychees are delicious when combined with other tropical fruits in salads. They can also be cooked in sweet syrup and canned. Dried lychees are shriveled but moist and tasty.

Borne in clusters, lychees have a gelatinous, sweet white interior.

LYCHEE VARIETIES

Variety	Fruit description	Ripening season*	Comments
'Bengal'	Large, bright red, borne in clusters of 8–30, large seed.	June	Large, very vigorous tree. Easy to grow.
'Brewster'	Medium, bright red, spiny, borne in clusters of 6–20, large seed.	June–July	Large, vigorous, upright tree. One of the hardier varieties.
'Emperor'	Large, red, big seed.	June–July	One of the largest fruits, up to golf ball size. Often produces aborted (chicken tongue) seeds. Small tree, good for gardens.
'Groff'	Small, dull red, spiny, borne in clusters of 20–40, small seed.	Aug–Sept	Latest-ripening variety. Upright tree.
'Hak Ip'	Medium, dark red, smooth, borne in clusters of 15–25, large seed.	July	Slow-growing, compact tree with spreading branches.
'Kaimana'	Medium to large, red, borne in large clusters, excellent flavor.	June–July	Commercial variety in Hawaii; poor elsewhere.
'Kwai May Pink' ('Bosworth 3')	Small, pinkish red, borne in clusters, small seed, excellent quality.	June	Dependable producer.
'Kwai Mi' ('Kuei Wei', 'Kwai May Red')	Small, bright red, slightly spiny, borne in clusters of 15–30, large seed.	May–June	Large, spreading tree with brittle branches.
'Mauritius'	Medium, bright red, smooth, borne in clusters of 15–30, large seed.	May–June	Vigorous, spreading tree with weak branches. Cold sensitive.
'No Mai Tsz' ('No Mai Tze', 'No Mai Chi')	Medium, bright reddish yellow, borne in clusters of 10–25, small seed, brittle skin.	July	Poor in Hawaii. Slow-growing, spreading tree.
'Ohia'	Small to medium, yellow-red, small seed, excellent flavor.	June–July	Productive in Florida.
'Sweet Cliff'	Small, pinkish yellow to red, borne in clusters of 4–8, small to medium seed.	June	Recommended for Florida. Poor in alkaline soils. Small, slow-growing tree.
'Sweet Heart'	Large, red, excellent quality, small seed.	May–June	Good in Florida. Consistent producer. Often produces aborted (chicken tongue) seeds.

Harvest dates are for Florida and Hawaii. Fruits will ripen three to four months later in California.

Mango
Mangifera indica

- **Features: Evergeen tree, beautiful foliage, colorful flowers, delicious fruit**
- **Size: 25–50'H×20–30'W**
- **Hardiness: Young trees 30°F, mature trees 25°F**
- **Harvest: May to July in Florida and Hawaii, October to February in California**

Native to India and Southeast Asia, the mango is the apple of the tropics. Mangoes have long been one of the most commonly eaten fruits in tropical countries around the world. They are increasingly popular in North America, where they are available in supermarkets almost all year.

Mangoes vary in shape, size, and color. They can be round, oblong, or kidney shape and may have a small, pointed beak. They can weigh as little as 4 to 5 ounces or as much as 2 pounds. The skin color can be green, yellow, red, or purple, but usually it is a combination of several shades. The flesh is yellow to orange and when perfectly ripe has the texture of a peach. The flavor resembles that of peach, but it has a distinctive tropical sweetness.

The two types of mangoes are Indian and Indo-Chinese. Indian mangoes usually have brightly colored fruits, are susceptible to anthracnose, and produce seeds that do not grow true to type; they are the ones most often grown commercially in Florida. Indo-Chinese mangoes usually do not develop brightly colored fruits, but the trees are resistant to anthracnose; they usually produce seedlings identical to the parent.

There are many varieties of mangoes. Those described in the charts were selected for disease resistance, low fiber content, flavor, and long harvest season.

Some mangoes do not fall clearly into either category. These naturally occurring seedlings are found in the tropics. Some of

Ripe mangoes vary in shape and color.

them, such as 'Julie', are named cultivated varieties.

Most mangoes have a tendency to bear heavily in alternate years. To minimize alternate bearing, thin the fruit and fertilize more in a heavy crop year.

Adaptation Grow mango in relatively frost-free climates. Flowers and small fruit can be killed if temperatures drop below 40°F, even if for only a short period. Young trees may be seriously damaged if the temperature drops below 30°F, but mature trees may withstand very short periods of temperatures as low as 25°F. In Florida and Hawaii resistance to anthracnose, which damages flowers and fruit, is often the most important aspect of variety selection.

Mango must have warm, dry weather to set fruit. The tree seldom exceeds 25 feet tall in California, where the first bloom of the season usually occurs during cool, wet spring weather and results in poor fruit set. Later in the summer the second growth flush and bloom produce a crop that ripens in fall and winter.

The varieties in the chart on page 99 are adaptable to hot, dry summers and cold, wet winters; they are susceptible to anthracnose. However, removing the winter flower sprays forces new flowers to develop when conditions are drier and warmer and thus the fruit is not affected.

Mango flowers are borne on long stalks.

Other varieties commonly grown in California are listed at the bottom of the chart.

Mangoes are also grown in South Texas, but variety availability is limited. 'Manila' and 'Julie' are recommended for better flavor than common commercial varieties such as 'Haden' and 'Keitt'.

Pollination Mangoes are self-fruitful, but the amount of fruit set depends largely on warm temperatures, low humidity, and the activity of pollinating insects. Wet, humid weather favors anthracnose and poor fruit set. Temperatures below 55°F drastically reduce insect activity and limit pollination.

Propagation Indo-Chinese mangoes produce two or more seedlings from each seed. Because most of these seedlings are identical to the parent, Indo-Chinese mangoes are commonly grown from seed.

To grow mangoes from seed, remove the husk and plant the seed (before it dries out) with the hump at soil level. Transplant the seedling carefully, making sure not to sever the taproot.

Although most Indo-Chinese seedlings are true to type, some may be quite different from the parent, so for best results plant grafted or budded trees. If you want to graft your own trees, do it when the tree is in a growth flush.

Site selection and planting Mango

grows best in full sun and well-drained soil with a pH between 5.5 and 7.5. When planting a mango, take care not to damage the taproot.

■ **Mango in the landscape** Mango makes a handsome specimen or shade tree. Dwarf varieties, such as 'Fairchild' and 'Julie', can be grown in large pots. Mango leaves are long, narrow, and lustrous deep green. The new growth, which comes in flushes, is often tinged with red. The yellow to red flowers are borne in terminal sprays. Although each flower cluster may have hundreds of blooms, only a few will set fruit.

As a result the fruits dangle at the ends of stringlike stalks.

■ **Caring for mango**

■ **Watering** A tree requires consistent moisture to produce high-quality fruit. Water regularly in areas with low annual rainfall.

■ **Fertilizing** Regular applications of nitrogen fertilizer will promote healthy growth flushes and flower production. Follow the feeding program recommended for citrus (see page 44). Chelated micronutrients, especially iron, are also often necessary.

■ **Pruning** A healthy tree requires little pruning, although pruning to stimulate new growth will promote uniform annual bearing. Removing some flower clusters during a heavy bloom year may alleviate alternate bearing. You can prune a mango to control size in late winter or early spring without losing fruit.

■ **Pests and diseases** Fungal diseases, including anthracnose,

'Keitt' is a popular mango in Florida.

'Nam Doc Mai' mango

MANGO VARIETIES FOR FLORIDA

Variety	Fruit description	Ripening season	Comments*
'Alphonso'	Large, golden yellow, pleasant sweet-tart, almost fiberless.	June–July	Vigorous, large tree.
'Bailey's Marvel'	Medium to large, peach over yellow, tangy and sweet, fiberless.	July–Aug	Vigorous, round tree. Good cold hardiness.
'Edward'	Large, oval, golden yellow with red blush when exposed, aromatic, excellent sweet-tart flavor, fiberless.	May–July	(M) One of the best Florida varieties. Large, vigorous grower. Fruit turns yellow at base when ripe.
'Florigon'	Medium, yellow, fiberless, excellent flavor.	May–July	(P) Upright, rounded, very productive tree.
'Glenn'	Medium to large, oval, yellow to pink to red, rich, peachy flavor, fiberless.	late May–June	(M) Medium tree, productive, easy to grow.
'Haden'	Medium to large, deep yellow with a crimson blush, excellent eating, slightly fibrous.	May–July	(M) Old selection still preferred by some despite susceptibility to anthracnose.
'Keitt'	Very large, green with red blush, firm, small seed, excellent flavor, minimal fiber.	Aug–Sept	(M) Small to medium tree, very productive. Openness makes it less desirable in the landscape. Fruit often used green, pickled.
'Nam Doc Mai'	Large, yellow, aromatic, superb flavor.	June–July	(P) Highly regarded variety from Thailand. Small tree, moderately susceptable to anthracnose.
'Philippine'	Small, yellow, aromatic, rich sweet flavor, fiberless.	June–July	From Cuba. Known as 'Manila' in Mexico, 'Carabo' in Philippines.
'Tommy Atkins'	Large, yellow-orange with deep red blush, firm, small seed, good flavor.	June–July	Dense, rounded tree. Moderately resistant to anthracnose.

*M – monoembryonic (seedlings not true to type); P – polyembryonic (seedlings true to type)

Mango *(continued)*

powdery mildew, and scab, can be serious problems in Florida and Hawaii. Consult your local cooperative extension service for preventive measures. Unless otherwise mentioned varieties described in the Hawaii and Florida charts have good anthracnose resistance. Mangoes listed in the California chart

'Early Gold' mango

'Peggy Winters' mango

MANGO VARIETIES FOR HAWAII

Variety	Fruit description	Ripening season	Comments*
'Ah Ping'	Large, yellow and orange, small seed, good quality, fiberless.	July	(M) Upright, productive tree.
'Ataulfo'	Small, S-shape, greenish to yellow, thin seed, delicious rich flavor, almost fiberless.	Mar–July	
'Brook's Late'	Medium to large, green, mild sweet flavor.	Aug–Oct	Florida selection, tolerates wet conditions.
'Excel'	Medium, red and yellow, fine flavor, low fiber.	July–Aug	Best in drier areas, susceptible to anthracnose.
'Fairchild'	Small, greenish yellow with orange-yellow blush, medium to large seed, mild sweet flavor, almost fiberless.	June–July	(P) Small, spreading tree bears lightly. Widely adapted, good for smaller gardens and containers.
'Glenn'	Medium to large, yellow with orange-red blush, excellent quality.	June–July	(M) Small to medium tree, can be pruned to maintain small size. Almost fiberless fruits.
'Gouveia'	Large, light green mottled red and yellow, small seed, rich acidic flavor, almost fiberless.	July–Aug	(M) Upright tree. Best in drier areas, susceptible to anthracnose.
'Haden'	Large, round to oval, juicy, good flavor, medium fiber.	late May–early July	(M) Vigorous, spreading tree. Best in drier areas; susceptible to anthracnose. Alternate bearing.
'Julie'	Small, dark green and red, good flavor, almost fiberless.	Aug–Sept	(M) Small, slow-growing tree. Susceptible to anthracnose.
'Keitt'	Very large, green with red blush, firm, small seed, excellent flavor, minimal fiber.	Aug–Sept	(M) Small to medium tree, very productive. Openness makes it less desirable in the landscape. Fruit often used green, pickled.
'Kensington Pride'	Medium to large, yellow-green with light blush, excellent flavor, medium fiber.	June–July	(P) Vigorous, spreading tree.
'Momi K'	Small to medium, light yellow with light orange-red blush, mild flavor, low fiber.	June–Aug	(M) Irregular bearing. Medium to large, spreading canopy.
'Pope'	Medium, green-yellow with reddish pink blush, excellent spicy flavor.	July–Aug	(M) Heavy bearing in alternate years.
'Rapozo'	Very large, yellow-orange with red blush, excellent quality, fiberless.	Aug–Oct	(M) Medium tree, productive.
'White Pirie'	Small to medium, greenish yellow, good quality.	July	Old Hawaiian variety. Spreading tree.

*M – monoembryonic (seedlings not true to type); P – polyembryonic (seedlings true to type)

are generally susceptible to anthracnose. Mites, mealybugs, thrips, and scale insects can be occasional problems. Mexican, Mediterranean, and Oriental fruit flies may be serious pests in Hawaii and in the Southeast.

▌ **Harvest and storage** Mango fruits are ready to pick 100 to 150 days after flowering. The fruits take less time to mature and have the best flavor if allowed to ripen on the tree. Ripe fruit turns the characteristic color of the variety and begins to soften to the touch, much as a peach does. Unripe fruit tastes like turpentine.

Pick mature, well-colored, firm fruit and ripen it at room temperature or store it for 20 to 25 days at a cool temperature but not below 55°F.

▌ **Mango at the table** Mango can be cut into large chunks provided the fruit is ripe and your knife is sharp.

To peel and seed a mango, make four longitudinal cuts in the skin and remove the sections of the peel as you would peel a banana. Then cut the flesh in slices parallel to the seed. Eat the slices out of hand, use them in a mango salad, or let them marinate in Sauterne and lime juice and serve chilled as a superb dessert.

Use underripe mango in duck or pork stew. Add ripe mango to breads, ice cream, sorbets, tarts, and chutneys.

This heavy crop of mangoes needs thinning to produce quality fruit.

'Kensington Pride' mango

MANGO VARIETIES FOR CALIFORNIA**

Variety	Fruit description	Ripening season	Comments*
'Aloha'	Small to large, red, sweet flavor, small seed, almost fiberless.	Nov–Dec	Spreading tree bears lightly.
'Edgehill'	Small to medium, green with red blush, sweet flavor, almost fiberless.	Dec–Feb	Upright tree.
'Kenny'	Small, yellow, green, and pink, sweet flavor, fiberless.	Oct–Nov	Rounded tree bears lightly.
'Manila'	Small, yellow, small seed, fiberless.	Oct–Dec	(P) Large bushy shrub.
'Piña'	Small, yellow and orange, sweet flavor, almost fiberless.	Nov–Dec	(P) Upright tree.
'Reliable'	Small to large, red and yellow, sweet, small seed, almost fiberless.	Dec–Jan	Dome-shape tree.
'Surprise'	Small to large, red and yellow, sweet flavor, small seed, fiberless.	Oct–Dec	Upright tree.
'T-1'	Medium to large, red, yellow, and green, sweet, small seed, fiberless.	Dec–Jan	Upright, rounded tree.
'Thomson'	Small to medium, yellow, sweet flavor, small seed, fiberless.	Dec–Jan	(P) Spreading tree.
'Villaseñor'	Medium, light green with pink blush, sweet flavor, small seed, fiberless.	Dec–Jan	Spreading tree. Moderately resistant to anthracnose.
'20222' ('Winters')	Small to medium, red and yellow, sweet flavor, fiberless.	Oct–Nov	(P) Dome-shape tree bears lightly.

*P – polyembryonic (seedlings true to type)
**Other varieties for California: 'Ataulfo', 'Glenn', 'Haden', 'Julie', 'Keitt', 'Kensington Pride', 'Kent', 'Nam Doc Mai', and 'Valencia Pride'.

Olive

Olea europaea

- **Features: Evergreen trees, silver-gray foliage, pungent fruits**
- **Size: 20–30'H×20–30'W**
- **Hardiness: 12°F**
- **Harvest: Fall into early winter**

A classic Mediterranean fruit tree, olive has been grown in the West from the early days of the Spanish missions. Its silvery foliage and gnarled trunk are a familiar sight in home landscapes and agricultural areas of California and the Southwest. In home gardens olive is more commonly grown as an ornamental than as a fruit tree. Because the fruits are difficult to pick, they need to be processed before they can be eaten, and large quantities are required to press for oil.

Adaptation Olive is supremely adapted to areas with long dry summers. In general it does not perform well in the wet, humid summers of the Southeast but is occasionally grown in drier parts of Hawaii. The tree is hardy to about 12°F. Green fruits are damaged at about 28°F, but ripe fruits withstand somewhat lower temperatures. Hot, dry winds during bloom may affect fruit set. Most varieties perform best with at least 300 hours of chilling.

Pollination Olive trees produce two kinds of flowers: a perfect flower containing both male and female parts, and a staminate (male) flower with pollen-producing stamens only. The perfect flowers are largely wind pollinated. Most olive varieties are self-fertile, although fruit set is usually improved by cross-pollination with other varieties. Some varieties are self-sterile and do not set fruit unless pollinated by other varieties, and some varieties are not good pollinators. Environmental factors such as high temperatures may also cause pollination problems.

Propagation Propagate olives from cuttings or graft named varieties onto seedling rootstocks (see "Grafting and budding on pages 29 and 30). Seedlings are highly variable.

Site selection and planting An olive can be grown in almost any well-drained soil up to pH 8.5. The tree is tolerant of mildly saline conditions.

Olive in the landscape Olives are beautiful trees; their glistening foliage and handsome branching make a perfect silvery accent or focal point in any landscape. They can also be grown in containers and pruned as espaliers. However, unpicked fruit drops to the ground and makes a mess on patios or paving. Fruitless varieties such as 'Swan Hill' are available;

Olives come in a variety of shapes, sizes, and colors.

'Kalamata'

'Alfonso'

'Nyan'

'LaCatalina'

'Cerignola'

'Niçoise'

'Gaeta'

'Abequina'

they produce little pollen, ideal for allergy sufferers who are bothered by the abundant pollen from olive trees. Olive trees can be sprayed during bloom to prevent fruit set. For more information, consult a local nursery or your cooperative extension service.

■ **Caring for olives** Olive trees can survive with little care if grown strictly as an ornamental, but high-quality crops of fruit require regular watering and pruning.

■ **Watering** Olives are drought tolerant once established. In dry regions once-a-month deep watering will ensure good yields in heavy soils; a tree in sandy soil needs more frequent irrigation.

■ **Fertilizing** An olive tree seldom needs feeding.

■ **Pruning** Olives are usually grown as multitrunk trees. Proper pruning keeps a tree productive and easier to harvest. After planting select three scaffold branches and remove suckers, watersprouts, and damaged, or crossing branches. Flowers are borne on the previous year's growth, so encourage side branches for flower production. Light pruning stimulates vigorous

Like the lavender in the foreground, olive trees are well adapted to dry-summer California and Arizona.

Olives turn from green to purplish black as they mature.

new growth for flowering and fruiting, but drastic pruning reduces fruit production. Avoid alternate bearing with careful pruning and fruit thinning.

Olive trees create a shady retreat.

■ **Pests and diseases** Olives have few serious pests when grown in full sun and well-drained soil. However, olive fruit fly can ruin fruit crops in most of California. For control measures, consult your local cooperative extension service. Olives are susceptible to verticillium wilt, a serious fungal disease in California. Control is difficult, so avoid planting in soils where verticillium is known to exist.

■ **Harvest and storage** Olives generally turn blackish purple when fully ripe but are often picked earlier at a green mature stage. A few varieties are ripe when green, and some turn a shade of coppery brown. Varieties vary considerably in size, oil content, and flavor. They also range in shape from almost round to oval or elongated with pointed ends.

Green mature fruits are pickled for green salad olives or allowed to completely ripen to the black stage

Olive *(continued)*

Olive's silvery green foliage and open, multitrunk habit create a rugged look, ideal for western gardens.

on the tree for crushing to extract olive oil or for making salted black olives. Ripe olives bruise easily and should be handled with care. Mold is a major problem between picking and curing.

Raw olives contain an alkaloid that makes them bitter and unpalatable. Traditionally olives were treated with lye and bathed in water to remove bitterness. The caustic nature of lye, however, makes the following method preferable and more environmentally friendly.

▮ **Salt curing** Rinse the olives with water, puncture them with a fork to increase penetration of the brine, and place them into a large clay crock or glass jar. Cover with brine made with ½ cup of coarse salt to 10 cups of water. Be sure that the olives are fully submerged. Drain daily and replace with fresh brine. Continue for 10 days for black olives or 12 days for green olives. Taste a sample to see if the bitterness is gone.

▮ **Storing cured olives** Make a brine using 1 cup of coarse salt to 10 cups of water; bring to a boil to dissolve the salt, then allow the solution to cool. Pack the olives in jars and cover with brine, leaving ½ inch at the top for a thin layer of olive oil to prevent air infiltration. Seal each jar with a lid. The olives should keep for up to a year.

About 24 hours prior to serving, drain the brine from the jar and replace it with cold water. Store the jars in the refrigerator. If the olives are too salty, repeat the process using warm water. Add spices such as garlic, rosemary, or hot peppers for flavor.

Salt-cured olives can keep up to a year.

OLIVE VARIETIES

Variety	Fruit description	Comments
'Ascalano'	Very large fruit, small pit, light green even when ripe, not as bitter as the other varieties.	Productive. One of the best for processing.
'Manzanillo'	Very large fruit, high oil content, ripens early.	Vigorous and productive. Good for processing.
'Mission'	Medium fruit, freestone, very bitter, ripens late.	Vigorous, heavy bearing. Cold resistant. Good all-purpose olive variety.
'Picholine'	Large fruit, elongated, delicate flavor.	Vigorous, productive. Excellent for green olives and oil. Cold resistant.
'Sevillano'	Very large fruit, large seed, low oil, tough flesh.	Fair for canning.

Papaya

Carica spp.

- **Features:** Upright woody perennial, beautiful tropical foliage, delicious fruit
- **Size:** 6–20'H×6–10'W
- **Hardiness:** Frost-free climates
- **Harvest:** 3 to 4 months after pollination in warm climates, twice as long in cooler areas

'Solo' is the most widely grown Hawaiian papaya variety.

Papaya adds a distinctive tropical appearance to landscapes.

Native to Central America, papaya is an unbranched, single-stem perennial that grows to a height of 6 to 20 feet. Its deeply lobed, dark green leaves have a boldly tropical look and reach 2 feet wide in ideal conditions.

The three types of papayas are Hawaiian *(C. papaya),* Mexican *(C. pubescens),* and babaco *(C. pentagona).* Hawaiian papayas are the ones commonly found in supermarkets. These pear-shape fruits are about 6 inches long, generally weigh about a pound, and have a yellow skin when ripe. The flesh is bright orange or pinkish, depending on variety, with small black seeds clustered in the center. 'Solo', the most common variety, has orange flesh. 'Sunrise' has light pink flesh, and 'Sunset' orange-red flesh. Others include 'Kamiya', 'Kapoho', 'Vista Solo', and 'Waimanalo', all with orange-yellow flesh. All varieties have a pleasant, sweet flavor. Hawaiian papayas are easy to harvest because the plants seldom grow taller than 8 feet.

Mexican papayas are much larger than Hawaiian: They weigh up to 10 pounds and can exceed 15 inches in length. The flesh may be yellow, orange, or pink. Their flavor is less intense than that of Hawaiian papaya but still delicious. They are slightly easier to grow than Hawaiian papayas.

Babaco develops long, pointed, seedless fruits (about 12 inches long) with yellow, melon-flavor flesh. Though hardier than papaya, it needs warm winters and part shade in areas with hot summers. Because it is small in stature and self-fruitful, babaco is ideally suited to container culture.

Papaya plants grow quickly and begin producing fruit within a year of germination. Replace the plant every three or four years, because the fruit quality declines as the plant ages.

Adaptation A papaya has exacting climate requirements for vigorous growth and fruit production. It must have warmth all year and is damaged by light frosts. Cold, wet soil is almost always lethal. Grow plants in containers or raised beds in areas with cool, rainy winter weather. Cool temperatures alter fruit flavor. For most of North America, papaya culture is limited to the greenhouse.

Pollination The plants have a unique flowering habit. They may produce only female flowers, only male flowers, or both. To complicate matters, a plant may change from one form to another during its life cycle. In any case male and female flowers must be present to produce fruit, so plant at least three or four plants in a group to ensure pollination. The illustrations at left will help you

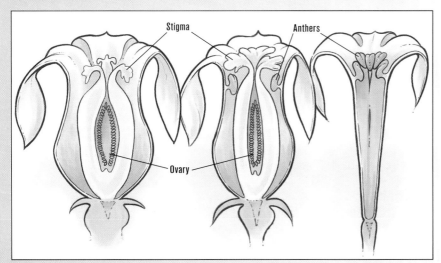

Papaya flowers may be female only (left), contain both the male and female flower parts (center), or be male only (right).

Papaya *(continued)*

Mexican papaya bears large fruits, up to 10 pounds.

Papayas ripen from the bottom to the top of the main stem.

identify which types of flowers your plants have.

Some varieties tend to produce certain types of flowers. For example, 'Solo' seedlings have flowers of both sexes 66 percent of the time, so two out of three plants will produce fruit even if they are planted singly.

▌ **Propagation** Most papaya plants are grown from seed. Extract the seeds from a ripe fruit. Wash the seeds to remove the gelatinous covering, and plant them immediately in warm (80°F), sterile potting mix. The seeds lose their viability rapidly in storage. Germination occurs in 10 to 15 days. Because seedling papaya does not transplant well, start the seeds in large containers so that you'll have to transplant only once, when you move the plants into the ground. Transplant carefully, making sure not to damage the root ball.

Propagating papaya from semihardwood cuttings is difficult and rarely done for types that grow well from seed.

▌ **Site selection and planting** Choose a planting site with a great deal of heat and sun. If possible plant along a south-facing wall. Well-drained soil is also essential; excess moisture can kill papayas. Many gardeners go to great lengths to provide excellent drainage, such as installing drain tiles and planting in containers or raised beds. Papaya plants do not tolerate salty water or saline soil.

Avoid breaking the root ball when planting. Set the plants a little high to allow for settling. Use mulch, but keep it away from the trunk. Black plastic mulch will help keep the soil warm and dry in wet-winter areas; remove it as soon as the weather warms up.

In hot inland areas of California, some gardeners have had luck treating smaller varieties as annuals; they plant seeds in fall, grow the plants over winter in a warm greenhouse, and then transplant them outdoors when the weather has warmed in spring. The fruit ripens that fall.

▌ **Papayas in the landscape** With large, deeply lobed leaves and an upright growth habit, papayas rank alongside bananas for unmatched tropical appearance. Use them as background plants or focal points. They look particularly good combined with other tropical plants around pools or patios, and they adapt well to growing in containers.

Babaco is self-fruitful and is usually propagated from cuttings.

Papayas are easy to start from seeds.

■ Caring for papaya

■ **Watering** This is the most critical aspect of raising papayas. Provided soil drainage is good, water the root zone regularly to prevent the leaves from wilting during warm weather. Keep the plant on the dry side to avoid root rot during cool weather.

■ **Fertilizing** Papaya requires regular applications of nitrogen fertilizer, but the exact rates have not been established. Feed monthly with a complete fertilizer and adjust the rate according to the plants' response. Plants also benefit from regular applications of micronutrients.

■ **Pruning** Papayas do not need to be pruned, but some growers pinch the seedlings or cut back established plants to encourage multiple trunks.

■ **Pests and diseases** Fruit flies can ruin fruit in Hawaii and Florida. Consult the local cooperative extension service for control measures. Thrips, mites, and whiteflies are potential problems in some areas, as are powdery mildew, anthracnose, and various virus diseases. Avoid root rot and nematodes by planting in well-drained soil.

■ **Harvest and storage** Pick papaya when most of the fruit's skin is yellow-green. After several days of ripening at room temperature, it should be almost fully yellow and slightly soft to the touch. Dark green fruit will not ripen properly off the tree, even though it may turn yellow on the outside, and it will not contain viable seeds. Fully mature fruits will have edible dark brown to black seeds the size of small peas completely filling the internal cavity. You can store mature fruits at 45°F for about three weeks.

■ **Papaya at the table** Combined with mango, peach, Indian spices, citrus, sugar, and vinegar, papaya makes a chutney that enhances a myriad of dishes including curry, meat kabobs, pork, and game. But the papaya is so beautiful, sweet, and fragrant that creative cooks also use it in simple dishes that don't require cooking.

Papaya is incredibly versatile. Here are just a few ideas: served with cured ham; pared, sliced, spread into a fan, and served with a few of its seeds on a bed of watercress with a wedge of lime; sliced and pared with smoked duck, toasted walnuts, and a walnut oil vinaigrette; filled with aioli (homemade mayonnaise with crushed garlic), shredded chicken, and cilantro; cut in chunks paired with scallops and tossed with Greek lemon sauce; chopped in Southwestern salsa; and desserts such as in mousse, or in pie, served with candied ginger bits, or pureed in a food mill, mixed with a little lime juice, and poured over ice cream.

The seeds have a spicy flavor that complements many sauces and salad dressings.

The fruit contains an enzyme called papain, which is sold as a meat tenderizer and natural antacid. Papaya is also rich in vitamins A and C, and some say it aids digestion.

Sliced papaya reveals rich-tasting flesh and black seeds.

Passionfruit

Purple granadilla
Passiflora spp.

- **Features: Vigorous evergreen or semi-evergreen vine, stunning flowers, attractive foliage, exotic fruit**
- **Size: 15–30'H×10–25'W**
- **Hardiness: Relatively frost-free climate depending on variety**
- **Harvest: 60 to 80 days after flowering**

Passionfruit is a member of a large family of vining plants, many of which are grown as ornamentals for their beautiful flowers and delicate leaves. Several species and varieties produce edible fruit, but the most widely available is the purple granadilla, *P. edulis,* and its hybrids.

Native to tropical America, passionfruit was named by Spanish missionaries to whom its intricate and strikingly beautiful flowers represented the Passion of Christ. The blooms are 2 to 3 inches in diameter with white petals and numerous hairlike filaments that are purple and white.

The fruits are egg-shape, 2 to 5 inches in diameter, and purple to reddish purple when ripe. The rind is inedible. The yellowish green to yellowish orange pulp surrounds small black seeds, which most people strain out before using the juice or flavoring. However, the seeds are edible.

Passionfruit vine has glossy green leaves with three lobes and serrated edges. The tendrils cling to almost any support. The vine grows extremely quickly and requires heavy pruning to keep it in bounds.

Adaptation Passionfruit does best in frost-free climates, although it may survive for short periods at temperatures below freezing. The vine may lose some of its leaves in cool winters, and the roots may resprout if the top is killed. Passionfruit does not grow well in intense summer heat. Vines are

Fruits of yellow passionfruit stand out against their supporting trellis.

short-lived and should be replaced every 5 to 7 years.

Pollination Purple granadilla is self-fruitful, but pollination is best under humid conditions. Some other species may require cross-pollination (see page 107).

Propagation Passionfruit is usually propagated from semihardwood cuttings. Be sure to propagate only healthy-looking, disease-free plants. Fresh seeds from superior fruits usually produce vines with good fruit. Seeds germinate in 10 to 20 days; they should not be exposed to light during germination. Seeds stored for more than 8 to 12 months lose viability.

Site selection and planting Excellent drainage is absolutely necessary.

The soil should be rich in organic matter and low in salts. Because the vines are shallow rooted, they benefit from a thick layer of organic mulch. Plant in full sun except in very hot areas, where partial shade is preferable. Plant next to a chain-link fence or install a strong trellis before planting to provide a framework for the vine to climb on.

Passionfruit in the landscape An excellent ornamental that can be grown on a fence, trellis, or any kind of sturdy support, passionfruit must be regularly pruned or it can overwhelm even a strong structure. Include a trellis or other support for the vine if you grow it in a container.

Caring for passionfruit

Watering The plant must have consistent moisture or the harvest will be smaller and the fruit quality poorer.

Fertilizing The vigorous passionfruit vine requires regular applications of a balanced fertilizer. Too much nitrogen, however, results in vigorous foliage growth at the expense of flowers and fruit.

Pruning You'll have to prune to keep the vine within bounds and to make harvesting easy. In warm-winter climates prune

Purple granadilla bears deep purple fruits on a vigorous vine.

Passionfruit flowers exhibit the intricacy of their blossoms.

Cut passionfruit reveals its gelatinous flesh and seeds.

immediately after harvest. In areas with cool winters, prune in early spring. Fruiting occurs in the leaf joints of the current season's growth, so regular pruning to maintain vigorous growth from the main branches keeps the plants productive. As a general rule remove all weak growth and cut back vigorous growth by at least one-third. When left unpruned passionfruit vines will grow out of control and produce fruit well out of reach. However, in very hot climates allow a thick canopy of foliage to grow around the fruit to prevent sunburn.

■ Pests and diseases Snails can be a serious problem in California; they can completely strip a vine of leaves and bark, killing young plants or predisposing them to disease. Passionfruit is also susceptible to nematodes and viruses and other diseases that thrive in cool soils, such as fusarium.

■ Harvest and storage The fruits quickly turn from green to deep purple when ripe and then fall to the ground within a few days. Pick them when they change color or gather them from the ground each day.

To store passionfruits wash and dry them gently and place them in polyethylene bags. They should last two to three weeks at 50°F. Slightly shriveled fruit can still be eaten. Both the fruit and the juice freeze well.

■ Passionfruit at the table Cut passionfruit in half and scoop out the flesh with a spoon. Eat it as is, make jelly, or passionfruit juice. Use the juice in ice cream, butter, sorbet, and mousse or drink it alone or mixed with other fruit juices. It makes great marinade, dessert topping, and sauce.

PASSIONFRUIT SPECIES

Species	Fruit description	Flower description	Comments
P. alata, fragrant granadilla	Oval, 3–5", skin yellow, pulp white, aromatic, good flavor.	Large and fragrant. Red, green, and white.	Self-fruitful. Oval, unlobed leaves. Winged stems.
P. coccinea, red granadilla	Oval, 2", skin yellowish orange with green stripes, pulp white, sweet.	Scarlet to orange, pink, white, and purple. Hard and brittle at maturity.	Requires cross-pollination. Serrated leaves, no lobes.
P. edulis, purple granadilla	Oval, 2–3½", skin purple, pulp yellow, seeds black, highly aromatic, rich, sweet-tart flavor.	Large. White, green, and purple. Flowers open in morning, close by noon.	Self-fruitful. Leaves attractive, lobed, and deeply toothed. Improved hybrids include 'Black Knight', 'Edgehill', 'Frederick', 'Kahuna', 'Red Rover', and 'Purple Possum'.
P. edulis flavicarpa, yellow passionfruit	Round to oval, 2–3", skin yellow, flesh dark orange, seeds brown, fair quality, tart flavor.	Large. White and purple. Flowers open at noon during spring, summer, and fall.	May require cross-pollination. Selections exist but are rarely available.
P. incarnata, maypop	Oval, 2", yellow skin, tart apricot flavor.	White, lavender, and pinkish purple.	Deeply lobed, toothed leaves. Hardiest type. Native to the eastern United States. Dormant in winter.
P. laurifolia, yellow granadilla	Oval, 2–3½", skin lemon yellow to orange, pulp white, pear flavor.	Purple, blue, and rose.	Requires cross-pollination. Produces few flowers. Undivided leaves.
P. ligularis, sweet granadilla	Oval, 2½–4", skin purplish yellow, pulp white, distinctive sweet flavor.	Greenish white.	Best in cool climates. Excellent flavor.
P. maliformis, sweet calabash	Globe shape, 1½", skin yellowish green, pulp white, grape flavor.	Fragrant. White, red, and purple.	Self-fruitful. Long, narrow, undivided leaves.
P. mollissima, banana passionfruit	Oval, 2½", skin yellowish, flesh white, sweet-tart flavor.	White, pink, and purple.	Best in cool climates. Prized for making juice. Lobed, serrated leaves.
P. quadrangularis, giant granadilla	Oblong, 8–12", skin yellowish green with pink tint, pulp white to pink, mild flavor.	Fragrant. Reddish purple and white.	Large fruit weighs up to 1 pound. Whitish rind eaten like watermelon. Oval, unlobed leaves. May require hand pollination.

Persimmon

Japanese persimmon,
Oriental persimmon
Diospyros kaki

▪ **Features: Deciduous tree,**
brilliant fall foliage, tasty fruit
▪ **Size: 20–30'H×20–30'W**
▪ **Hardiness: 0°F**
▪ **Harvest: Fall to early winter**

Japanese persimmon can be grown outdoors in more areas than most other plants in this book. Native to Asia, the Japanese persimmon is a handsome tree that lights up the landscape in fall when its glossy, deep green leaves turn brilliant shades of yellow, orange, and red. When the leaves drop they reveal bright orange fruits dangling among the bare branches. The fruits, which range from the size of a baseball to a small grapefruit, can be round, heart-shape, flattened, or ridged.

The varieties of Japanese persimmon are divided into two types: astringent and nonastringent. Astringent fruit is inedible when hard and must be allowed to soften before it develops its full sweetness and flavor. A nonastringent variety can be eaten when hard, as soon as it develops its characteristic color. Persimmons are also classified as pollination variant and pollination constant. In pollination-variant types, the flesh is dark and streaked around the seeds, but clear orange when seedless. Pollination-constant types lack dark streaking regardless of seed set. In astringent cultivars of the pollination-variant type, the dark flesh is nonastringent even when hard, thus performing as nonastringent types. In most areas of the world astringent pollination-variant types are classified as nonastringent. However, these persimmons typically are grown without pollinators, and their seedless, astringent fruit necessitates classifying them as astringent types.

▪ **Adaptation** Japanese persimmon does best in areas that have moderate winters and relatively mild summers. It can tolerate 0°F when fully dormant, but because of its low chilling requirement (less than 100 hours), it may break dormancy during early warm spells only to be damaged by spring frosts later. It generally does not produce well in desert heat.

▪ **Pollination** Most of the varieties described here will set seedless fruit without being pollinated; when pollination does occur, the fruit will have seeds. Most named varieties produce only female flowers. When male flowers are present, the fruit is seedy. Most gardeners prefer seedless fruit, but some insist that persimmons develop peak flavor only when the fruit results from pollination.

▪ **Propagation** Japanese persimmon usually is budded or grafted to a seedling rootstock. Eastern nurseries often graft Japanese persimmon onto an American persimmon *(D. virginiana)* rootstock because of the native species' extra hardiness. This is not recommended in the southern United States where the American species has been ravaged by persimmon wilt. Consult your cooperative extension service for more information.

▪ **Site selection and planting** Full sun and well-drained soil with a pH range of 5 to 6.5 is ideal, but persimmon is fairly adaptable and can withstand a wide range of conditions as long as the soil is not overly salty.

American persimmon fruits
complement golden fall foliage.

A ripening 'Fuyu' persimmon dangles
among fall foliage.

▪ **Persimmon in the landscape** A superb small tree that looks good in all seasons, persimmon can be grown as a small shade tree, specimen, or background planting. Or prune it and use it as an informal hedge, screen, or espalier.

▪ **Caring for persimmon**

▪ **Watering** Persimmon trees can withstand short periods of drought, but the fruit will be larger and of higher quality with regular watering. Extreme drought causes the leaves and fruit to drop prematurely. Any fruit left on the tree will probably sunburn.

▪ **Fertilizing** Most trees do well with a minimum of fertilizing. Excess nitrogen can cause fruit drop. If the leaves are not deep green and shoot growth is less than a foot per year, apply a balanced fertilizer such as 10-10-10 at a rate of 1 pound per inch of trunk diameter at ground level. Spread it evenly under the canopy in late winter or early spring.

Japanese persimmons hang on the tree
after the leaves have dropped.

A cut Japanese persimmon reveals its succulent orange flesh.

■ **Pruning** Prune to develop a strong framework of main branches while the tree is young. Otherwise the fruit, which is borne at the tips of the brittle branches, may be too heavy and cause breakage. A mature Japanese persimmon requires little pruning other than removing broken or crisscrossing branches and suckers. Occasional fruit thinning reduces the load on the branches.

Even though the tree grows well on its own, it can be pruned heavily to create a hedge or a screen or to control size. It even makes a nice espalier.

■ **Pests and diseases** The plant is relatively problem free.

Persimmon wilt can be a serious problem for trees grafted onto American persimmon rootstocks in some areas of the South.
■ **Harvest and storage** Pick astringent varieties when they are hard but fully colored. They will soften on the tree and improve in quality, but you will probably lose many fruits to birds. Astringent persimmons will ripen off the tree if stored at room temperature. They are ready to eat when they soften to a pudding texture.

Nonastringent persimmons are ready to harvest when they are fully colored, but for best flavor allow them to soften slightly before harvest.

Cut both kinds of persimmons from the tree with handheld pruning shears, leaving the calyx (the leaflike collar) and a small piece of stem attached to the fruit. Even though the fruit is relatively hard when harvested, it bruises easily, so handle with care.

Mature, hard astringent persimmons can be stored in the refrigerator for at least a month. They can also be frozen for six to eight months. They will be soft

and ready to eat when thawed.

Nonastringent persimmons deteriorate quickly in the refrigerator, but they can be stored for a short period at room temperature.
■ **Persimmon at the table** Soft astringent fruits are delicious and attractive simply halved and eaten with a spoon. They are also a common ingredient in puddings, pies, and quick breads. Nonastringent varieties, which can be eaten hard, are good in salads, as an accompaniment to cured or game meats, or as a garnish. They are also quite enjoyable quartered and eaten plain. If you freeze astrigent fruits, they will lose their astringency. Eat them frozen or thaw to use in pudding or baked goods.
■ **Japanese persimmon relatives** The native tree, American persimmon *(D. virginiana),* can withstand –20°F. The tree is similar to Japanese persimmon but is slightly larger. The fruit is smaller and astringent, so it must be softened before it can be eaten. Plant two trees to ensure pollination and heavy yields.

JAPANESE PERSIMMON VARIETIES

Variety	Fruit description	Comments
'Chocolate'	Small, astringent pollen variant, skin reddish orange, flesh brown streaked when cross-pollinated, conical.	Named for flesh color. Vigorous, upright tree.
'Eureka'	Medium, astringent, bright red, flattened.	One of the best for Southern gardeners. Bears early, very productive. Vigorous, small, dense tree.
'Fuyu' ('Fuyugaki')	Medium, nonastringent, skin orangish red, flesh light orange, slightly flattened.	Tree vigorous, spreading. New growth has yellow tinge. 'Giant Fuyu' ('Gosho') resembles 'Fuyu' but bears inferior fruit.
'Giombo'	Large, early, astringent, light orange, conical, excellent flavor, conical.	One of the best flavored. Less hardy than other varieties.
'Hachiya'	Large, astringent, yellow-orange, heart shape.	One of the most common. Upright and slightly spreading.
'Izu'	Medium to large, early, astringent, fine flavor, conical.	Small tree.
'Maru'	Medium, astringent pollen variant type, orange-red, round.	Excellent quality.
'Nishumura Wase' ('Coffee Cake')	Medium to large, early, astringent pollen variant, orange, round, spicy flavor.	Productive. Usually sets male flowers.
'Saijo'	Small, early to midseason, astringent, yellow, conical.	One of the sweetest. Hardy, large, productive tree.
'Tamopan'	Large, astringent, orange-red, flattened acorn shape.	
'Tanenashi'	Medium, early, astringent, yellowish orange, conical.	Vigorous, rounded tree. Common in Florida.

Pomegranate

Punica granatum

- **Features:**
  Deciduous shrub or tree, brilliant fall foliage, showy flowers, tasty fruit
- **Size: 10–30'H×6–15'W**
- **Hardiness: 12°F**
- **Harvest: Fall**

Pomegranate originated in a region stretching from Iran to the Himalayas in northern India. Spanish missionaries brought it to the New World and planted it in their missions which expanded northward into California. The plant is an attractive, deciduous, rounded shrub to small tree that can reach 20 to 30 feet under ideal conditions. However, it is usually pruned to 10 to 12 feet high to keep it within bounds and to make harvesting easy. The thorny branches bear small, narrow, light green leaves that turn bright yellow in fall. New growth is tinged red. Showy orange-red flowers in spring are followed by colorful fruits in fall.

The 2½- to 5-inch rounded fruit features a prominent calyx (petallike projections) at the base. It has a tough, leathery skin that typically develops shades of pink to rich purplish red as it matures. The fruit's interior is separated into compartments like a honeycomb. A bitter spongy white membranous tissue surrounds sacs, each containing an angular seed with a soft to hard seed coat. The seed sac is filled with a red, pink, or whitish juicy pulp high in antioxidants. Varieties that produce fruit with hard seeds are considered inedible but are sometimes grown as ornamentals.

Adaptation Pomegranate is best adapted to arid regions of California and the Desert Southwest where long, hot summers and cool winters produce superior fruit. It is grown in the Southeast and Hawaii, often as an ornamental; fruit quality in humid climates is inferior.

Fine-texture, light green foliage, and bright orange-red blossoms make dwarf pomegranates useful ornamentals indoors and out.

Dormant plants are severely injured at 12°F and colder temperatures. Pomegranate seldom sets fruit in the northernmost limits of its range. The plant has a very low chilling requirement, so blooms are often killed by spring frosts.

Pollination Pomegranate is self-fruitful but will often bear more fruit if cross-pollinated.

Propagation Named selections are generally grown from hardwood or softwood cuttings. Seeds produce plants of highly variable fruit quality. Pomegranate may also be air layered. Grafting is not used as a method of propagation.

Pomegranate blossom

Site selection and planting A tough tree, pomegranate can survive under a variety of conditions. In mild-summer areas, such as the Pacific Northwest, plant in the warmest possible microclimate.

Pomegranate in the landscape Its handsome appearance makes it a good ornamental. Use it for a background planting, screen, or—because of its thorns—a security or barrier planting. You can grow it as a multitrunk tree, but you'll have to prune and remove suckers regularly to maintain its shape. Dwarf varieties such as 'Nana' (small but edible fruit) and 'Chico' (fruitless) make excellent container plants.

Caring for pomegranate

Watering Pomegranate is drought tolerant but should be watered regularly for best fruit quality. Almost-mature fruit will crack or split if the tree is allowed to undergo drought stress followed by rain or irrigation. Split fruit becomes moldy and is unusable.

Fertilizing Apply 1 pound of 10-10-10 in late winter (February–March) and early summer (June–July) when the plant is young.

Developing pomegranate fruits exhibit a characteristic prominent calyx at the base of the fruit.

Increase the rate as the plant grows until the mature tree is receiving 3 pounds of 10-10-10 twice a year.

Pruning Pomegranate may be grown as a bush or as a tree with one or more trunks. The bush form is satisfactory for backyards or hedgerows, but commercial orchards train their pomegranates as trees.

Allow four to six strong leaders to develop, evenly distributed around the trunk, to create a vase-shape scaffold branching system. Remove all other shoots.

Flowers are produced on short spurs (compact fruiting branches) found mostly on the outer edge of the tree, on two- or three-year-old wood. Light dormant pruning of mature trees encourages growth of new fruit spurs.

Cut leaders back to encourage new shoots on all sides and to prevent weak branches. The objective is to achieve a strong scaffold to support heavy crops and prevent limbs breaking.

Pests and diseases Relatively few pests and diseases present problems, but whiteflies, thrips, mealybugs, and scale insects can cause minor damage.

Alternaria fungus causes heart rot infection of the fruit.

'Wonderful' pomegranates light up the tree beginning in late summer.

Pomegranate (continued)

The infection occurs in the flower and progresses to the interior of the fruit. The rind is not affected by the fungus, but the central cavity can be partially or totally decayed. Infected fruit is difficult to detect. There is no known control. Hungry deer will feed on pomegranate foliage.

Harvest and storage The fruit matures about five to seven months after the plant flowers. Harvest in fall when the skin turns a distinctive yellow-orange to deep reddish purple; use handheld pruning shears to remove the fruit. Pomegranates do not continue to develop sugar after being picked. The fruit can be held in cold storage for up to seven months at 32° to 41°F and 80 to 85 percent relative humidity.

Refrigerate pomegranate juice and use it within two to three days after squeezing.

Pomegranate at the table The fruit can be eaten fresh or juiced. To remove the seeds cut the fruit into sections and peel back the skin to expose the juice-encapsulated seeds, which can be eaten whole. To juice the fruit simply cut it in half and use a citrus juicer. You can also roll the whole fruit on a hard surface to burst the juice sacs, insert a straw through a small hole in the skin, and suck out the juice.

Pomegranate seeds are delicious and colorful in salads. The juice can be used to make jams, jellies, and other preserves. It is also luscious fresh and in fruit smoothies and can be used in marinades and sauces.

When split open, pomegranate reveals its reddish purple edible seeds.

POMEGRANATE VARIETIES

Variety	Fruit description	Comments
'Ambrosia'	Very large, pale pink skin, purple juice, sweet-tart.	Fruits up to three times larger than 'Wonderful'.
'Christina'	Medium, deep red skin, pale pink seeds and juice.	Florida selection, reliable in the Southeast.
'Eversweet'	Medium, early, red skin, soft seeds, clear nonstaining juice, sweet.	Widely adapted. Seeds easy to eat.
'Fleishman'	Medium, pink skin and juice, very sweet.	Excellent quality. Pink flowers.
'Granada'	Small to medium, crimson skin, pink juice, tart.	Medium tree. Georgia selection.
'Plantation Sweet'	Medium to large, red skin and juice.	Small tree easily kept to 6' high. Good in pots.
'Red Silk'	Large, early, light greenish pink skin, pink juice, very sweet.	Productive, even when young.
'Sweet' ('Utah Sweet')	Medium, pink skin and juice, very sweet.	Softer seeds than 'Wonderful'.
'White'	Large, skin cream, tinged light pink, clear, nonstaining juice, sweet-tart.	Productive.
'Wonderful'	Large, deep purple-red skin and juice.	Most common variety. Good flavor but better for juicing than eating out of hand.

Tree Tomato

Tamarillo

Cyphomandra betacea

- **Features: Evergreen or semi-evergreen shrub or small tree, large leaves, small flowers, colorful egg-shape fruits**
- **Size: 10–12'H×6–10'W**
- **Hardiness: Frost-free climates**
- **Harvest: Fall to winter**

Immature tree tomato fruits resemble light green eggs.

Ripe fruits of tree tomato resemble purplish tomatoes.

Pepino resembles a small melon.

Native to the Peruvian Andes, the tree tomato is a member of the Solanaceae family, which includes many edible plants, such as eggplant, tomato, and potato. The fruit of the tree tomato faintly resembles the common garden tomato. Both red- and yellow-fruited types are available. Selected varieties are sometimes sold. The fruit is generally egg-shape and ranges from 1½ to 3 inches in diameter. A thin skin covers the orange flesh, which contains edible seeds. The flavor is sweet-tart, with the yellow type usually a little sweeter. Most people sweeten the fruit before eating it.

The tree tomato, which is partially deciduous in cold climates, produces large oblong leaves that may reach 10 inches long. It is usually grown from seeds or cuttings and is self-fruitful. Small pink flowers usually appear in late summer and fall but may come at almost any time. Tree tomato has long been grown as a houseplant.

Adaptation The foliage is damaged in a light frost, but the plant usually survives temperatures several degrees below freezing. Otherwise tree tomato is adaptable to a variety of climates.

Site selection and planting Tree tomato grows best in full sun except in hot, dry climates, where partial shade is better. It prefers a well-drained soil that is rich in organic matter. Protect the plant from strong winds.

Tree tomato in the landscape The large leaves, small flowers, and colorful fruit make tree tomato a useful landscape specimen, but it adapts well to container culture, indoors or outside.

Caring for tree tomato

Watering Tree tomato needs ample water during dry periods. Water regularly to promote vigorous growth. However, the plant can die within a few days if the soil remains saturated.

Fertilizing Feed regularly to keep the plant healthy. Apply half of the yearly fertilizer application in early spring and half in midsummer.

Pruning Pinch the plant when it is young to encourage branching, and as it matures prune to keep it from growing too tall. Fruit is borne on new growth, so prune out old branches to encourage new productive ones to develop.

Pests and diseases Aphids and nematodes are potential problems. Powdery mildew may also attack the foliage.

Harvest and storage The fruit is ready to harvest when it develops the yellow or red color characteristic of the variety. Simply pull the fruit from the tree with a snapping motion, leaving the 1- to 2-inch stem attached to the fruit. You can store tree tomatoes in the refrigerator for up to 10 weeks, but temperatures below 38°F can cause the skin to discolor.

Tree tomato at the table The fruit can be served fresh, cut in half, and eaten with a spoon, but most people prefer to sweeten it a little. Skin the fruit as you would a tomato by dipping it in boiling water for 20 to 30 seconds. The skin will then peel off easily. One easy method of serving is to slice the peeled fruit, sprinkle it with sugar to taste, and chill it overnight. The fruit also makes a good sauce for topping cheesecake, ice cream, or cake.

Tree tomato relatives Pepino (*Solanum muricatum*) is also known as melon shrub and melon pear. These names hint at the fruit's flavor: a combination of cantaloupe and honeydew melon. The oblong fruits are usually 2 to 6 inches long.

An upright, spreading plant 2 to 3 feet high, pepino has small bright blue flowers that will not set fruit unless night temperatures are above 65°F. It grows best in a moderate, humid climate with protection from hot sun.

The variety 'Toma' is popular. 'Corazona Oro', 'Peruvian Gold', 'Vista', 'Rio Bamba', and 'Misiki Prolific' are other selections that are sometimes available.

White Sapote

Mexican apple, zapote blanco

Casimiroa edulis

- **Features: Evergreen tree, handsome leaves, abundant good-tasting fruit**
- **Size: 25–60'H×25–30'W**
- **Hardiness: 24°F, flowers and fruit damaged by light frost**
- **Harvest: May through November in California, May to June or later in Florida**

White sapote has rich, smooth-texture white flesh.

'McDill' white sapote

Native to Mexico and Central America, white sapote is a distinctive large tree with glossy bright green leaves shaped like a hand. It produces an abundance of round greenish yellow or yellow fruits, 3 to 4 inches in diameter. The flesh has a smooth texture and sugary flavor reminiscent of peach or banana and contains three to five large seeds. Green-skinned varieties have white flesh. Yellow-skinned varieties have pale yellow flesh.

Adaptation Although the tree is hardy to 24°F, it blooms in late winter when frost may destroy flowers and young fruits. Young trees can be damaged at 30°F. White sapote does poorly in areas with high summer heat, such as the Southwest deserts, and in the high humidity of the tropical lowlands of Florida and Hawaii. It is well adapted to South and Central Florida and Southern California. It has been grown as far north as Chico, California. In cold areas, white sapote may be partially deciduous.

Propagation Fresh seeds will usually germinate in three to four weeks at 70° to 80°F. When the rootstock is ⅜ inch in diameter, it can be grafted or budded. Spring is the best time for grafting outdoors.

Pollination White sapote is generally self-fruitful but yields more if cross-pollinated.

Site selection and planting The tree prefers well-drained soil with a pH between 5.5 and 7.5, but it will grow in almost any soil as long as it is not overwatered and the drainage is good.

Before planting consider the mess made by unpicked fruit: Planting over a patio could be a big mistake, and raking fallen fruit from a lawn may be a bigger chore than you want.

White sapote in the landscape The tree's large size, greedy roots, and huge crop of fruit that often ends up on the ground make white sapote a poor landscape plant. It is best planted where it has plenty of room and doesn't become a nuisance.

Caring for white sapote

Watering Although the tree is drought tolerant, it produces better fruit with regular, deep watering, which is vital in keeping the greedy roots where they belong. Shallow watering encourages surface roots that will break pavement or ruin lawns. If you plant in a lawn, mulch under the tree canopy and water deeply.

Fertilizing White sapote requires regular applications of nitrogen fertilizer to maintain healthy growth. In years when the tree carries a heavy crop, apply a little extra nitrogen to help offset alternate bearing.

Pruning A young tree tends to grow vertically, without much branching. After planting pinch out the terminal bud to promote branching. A mature unpruned

White sapote fruits hang in clusters on large trees.

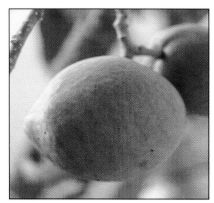

'Vernon' white sapote

white sapote tree produces such a huge crop that it is almost impossible for one family to pick it, let alone consume it. Unpicked fruit can be a problem because it drops from the tree as it ripens, making a mess and attracting bees and other insects. As the tree matures, prune it to encourage compact growth and to control size. Maintain the tree at 12 to 15 feet tall.

■ **Pests and diseases** White sapote has few serious pest or disease problems.

■ **Harvest and storage** Most varieties ripen over several weeks, but some, such as 'Suebelle', ripen over a much longer period, up to 6 months. Longer ripening is an advantage if you cannot use a lot of fruit all at once. A few varieties produce fruit year-round.

White sapote tastes best when tree ripened, but it bruises extremely easily. You must handle even green-stage fruits with care. Any bruised skin will turn black, and the underlying flesh will become bitter. Some varieties soften and develop good flavor if harvested at a hard/firm green mature stage, while others become bitter and inedible. Fruit changes color when ready to pick. Green varieties change from dark green to yellowish green; yellow varieties develop more intense yellow color. Fruits soften if picked too soon, but the flavor will be poor. Clip mature fruits from the branches leaving a short piece of stem attached. The stub will fall off when the fruit is ripe enough to eat.

Mature fruits will store for less than a week, but mashed pulp can be frozen and stored for 8 to 12 months.

■ **White sapote at the table** The best way to enjoy the fruit is to eat it fresh with a spoon, but you can mash the pulp and make it into an interesting sauce with a little lime or lemon juice. White sapote is also delicious in baked goods and sorbets.

WHITE SAPOTE VARIETIES

Species	Fruit description	Ripens	Comments*
'Blumenthal'	Medium, greenish yellow.	Sept–Nov	Recommended for South Florida. Must be cross-pollinated, plant with 'Dade'.
'Cuccio' ('Florida')	Medium, green.	Oct–Nov	Precocious tree, often bears second year after planting. Heavy producer.
'Dade'	Medium, yellowish green. Excellent quality, skin not bitter.	Sept–Oct	Recommended for South Florida. Must be cross-pollinated, plant with 'Blumenthal'.
'Denzler'	Small, yellow.	Oct–Dec	Recommended for Hawaii. Bears lightly, good dooryard tree.
'Ecke'	Small, bright yellow.	Oct–Nov	Skin colors up several weeks before ripening.
'Fiesta'	Small, thick, green.	Sept–Dec	Dependable producer.
'Lemon Gold'	Medium, round, smooth, light yellow, high quality.	Oct–Nov	Dependable producer. Attractive fruit keeps well, resists bruising. Can be picked immature and ripened off tree. Good pollenizer.
'Louise'	Small to medium, yellow, high quality.	Jan–Sept	Nearly everbearing in frost-free areas. Bears heavy crops.
'McDill'	Medium to large, round, yellowish green, excellent quality.	Nov–Dec	Vigorous tree bears early.
'Michele'	Small, light yellow, slight caramel flavor, good quality.	Apr–Nov	Small tree bears light crops.
'Pike'	Large, pointed, dark green. Thin, bitter skin.	Sept–Dec	Small, dependable tree.
'Suebelle'	Small to medium, light golden yellow, good quality.	July–Apr	Nearly everbearing in frost-free areas. Bears light crops.
'Vernon'	Medium to large, round, yellowish green.	Nov–Jan	Does well in coastal areas, even Northern California. Dependable producer.
'Vista'	Small, oblong, light yellow.	Oct–Nov	Tends to bear in alternate years.

Unless otherwise noted these varieties are best adapted to California.

Other Subtropical Fruits

This star fruit seedling will eventually bear fruits with five ribs.

Exotic dragonfruit, with bright pink flesh, black seeds, and sweet, melonlike flavor, is gaining popularity among subtropical fruit growers.

A tremendous number of plants will produce edible fruit in subtropical climates. The better ones that were not covered in the previous entries are discussed here. Two that have become quite popular are described in more detail. Others are listed alphabetically by botanical name in the chart that follows. They range in cold tolerance from the hardy pawpaw (*Asimina triloba*) to the sensitive acerola cherry (*Malpighia glabra*). Some species, such as pineapple, can be grown as houseplants.

▌ **Star fruit** Also known as carambola, the species *Averrhoa carambola* is native to Southeast Asia. It is an attractive small evergreen tree that grows about 20 to 30 feet high and wide under ideal conditions and can be trained to single or multiple trunks. In cooler climates it may lose most of its dark green divided leaves in winter or early spring. The light pink to lavender flower clusters are followed by yellow to orange fruits, 5 inches long with five lengthwise ridges. When cut across the fruit, the slices are star

shape, hence the name star fruit. The flavor ranges from very sour to sweet. The more commonly grown sweet varieties have a mildly sweet, watery, slightly acid taste with hints of citrus, pineapple, and apple.

Star fruit is widely grown in South Florida, Hawaii, and parts of Southern California. Established trees can survive brief spells of 26°F temperatures without damage, but they perform best in relatively frost-free winters. Young trees need protection because they can be killed at 32°F. Wind protection is necessary to prevent the tender fruits from scarring. Exterior fruit can also be damaged from sunburn. In the arid Southwest, plant star fruit where it will receive light afternoon shade.

A tree may produce several flushes of bloom; the main crop ripens from August to March in Florida and Hawaii, and from December to March in California. Selected varieties are usually self-fruitful, but cross-pollination may produce heavier crops.

Star fruit grows best in slightly acid (pH 5.5–6.5), well-drained, moist soils. It cannot tolerate drought. Feed regularly with a complete fertilizer. Pruning is usually not necessary.

Selected varieties are usually grafted. Seedling trees have unreliable fruit quality. Sweet varieties include 'Arkin', 'Fwang Tung' (requires a pollenizer), 'Golden Star', 'Kari', and 'Sri Kembanqan'.

The fruit is attractive and delicious in salads or floated in punch. It can also be eaten fresh.

▌ **Dragonfruit** What is sold as dragonfruit (also known as pitahaya or pitaya) is one of three species of the genus *Hylocereus* (*H. guatemalensis*, *H. polyrhizus*, and *H. undatus*), as well as hybrids of these species, and one species of *Selenicereus* (*S. megalanthus*). Native to Central and South America, these vining terrestrial or epiphytic cactus are evergreen plants that can climb 30 feet into trees using aerial roots to attach themselves as they go.

In gardens they are usually grown on a sturdy trellis or fence and are prized as ornamentals. Huge white flowers bloom at night and are pollinated by bats or bees in their native climates. Hand pollination increases fruit set in home gardens. Some varieties require pollen from another variety. The fruit is large (up to 1½ pounds), usually red, pink, or yellow with prominent scales. The flesh, which can be varying degrees of white, red, or magenta depending on the variety, usually has small black seeds. It has a sweet, often melonlike flavor and is highly nutritious.

Dragonfruit is damaged by light frosts but is well adapted to hot summer climates if given light shade. Plants suffer in prolonged cool weather. Flowers appear in cycles throughout the year but mainly in late summer. The fruit ripens four to eight weeks later. Dragonfruit is beautiful grown in a hanging basket or container. The stems, flowers, and fruit make a spectacular display cascading over the sides. It also does well indoors. Plants require regular water and fertilizer.

Plants are grown commercially in many areas of the tropics. They are often trellised on 6-foot-high posts that are firmly anchored in the ground; the posts are wrapped with burlap to provide support for epiphytic roots. A drip system supplies water and dilute soluble fertilizers directly to the roots.

Dragonfruit has become popular, with many new varieties being introduced from tropical climates. Seedling-grown varieties have unpredictable fruit quality. Plants are easily grown from cuttings that have been allowed to dry for 24 to 48 hours before planting.

Colorful fruit, fragrant flowers, and deep green foliage make natal plum an excellent landscape ornamental.

Pawpaw is hardy to −20°F and is also sometimes known as Michigan banana.

A ripe pineapple nestles on top of the plant's stiff, grassy foliage.

Jelly palm has blue-green leaves and clusters of edible fruits.

Other Subtropical Fruits *(continued)*

Varieties of *H. undatus,* which have triangular stems and few thorns, bear fruit with pink-red skin and white flesh. Popular varieties include 'Alice Snow', 'Cosmic Charlie', 'Dark Star', 'Neitzel', and 'Manny's Pink'. *H. polyrhizus* is thornier and bears fruit with pink skin and red flesh. 'Bloody Mary', 'Red Jaina', 'Zamorano', and 'Thompson' are selected varieties. *H. guatemalensis* 'American Beauty' is a fine-flavored variety with pinkish skin and green scales. It produces well without hand pollination.

The fruit of *S. megalanthus,* which has yellow skin and white flesh, is sweeter and smaller than the other types.

To eat dragonfruit fresh, chill it, cut it in half, and spoon out the flesh. You can use the juice for drinks, sorbets, and sauces.

Sliced star apple reveals the source of its common name.

Fruits of the coffee tree are deep red when ripe and contain two coffee beans each.

OTHER SUBTROPICAL FRUIT SPECIES

Species	Plant description	Fruit description	Comments
Ananas comosus, pineapple	Evergreen perennial 4' high, 6' wide. Rosettes of long, swordlike leaves have sharply toothed edges. Hardy to 28°F.	Oval, scaly texture, yellow with tones of brown, green, and orange. Sweet-tart flavor.	Good indoor plant where temperatures stay above 68°F. Grow from divisions or by rooting leafy top of fruit in moist sand or peat.
Asimina triloba, pawpaw	Deciduous shrubby tree 15–25' high, 10–15' wide. Purple flowers. Hardy to –25°F.	Shaped like a short, fat banana, 5–7" long, yellowish brown, sweet flesh, large seeds. Fruit falls to the ground when ripe.	Good for cold climates. Select grafted plants or grow from seed. Superior varieties include 'Davis', 'Mitchell', 'Overleese', 'Prolific', 'Sunflower', and 'Taytoo'. Some require cross pollination.
Butia capitata, jelly palm	Evergreen large 4–6', divided blue-green leaves. Heavy, thick trunk, reaches 15' high. Small cream to red flowers in long arching clusters. Hardy to 15°F.	Round, 1" diameter, long clusters, yellow to orange, pleasant, sweet-tart flavor.	Attractive ornamental. Fruit good for jelly or wine. Pick fruit as it ripens. Grown from seed, fruit quality variable.
Carissa macrocarpa, Natal plum	Handsome evergreen shrub, 6–12' high, 4–6' wide, thorny. Shiny green leaves, showy, fragrant white flowers. Hardy to 26°F.	Round, 1" diameter, red to purple, juicy red flesh, tart flavor.	Grow varieties selected for good fruit quality, such as 'Fancy', 'Torrey Pines', and 'Gifford'. Propagate by semihardwood cuttings. Drought tolerant.

Che turns red or reddish purple as it ripens.

Kei apple has yellow fruits and sharp thorns.

Surinam cherry fruits are red or black and ribbed.

Longan bears grapelike clusters of yellowish fruits.

OTHER SUBTROPICAL FRUIT SPECIES *(continued)*

Species	Plant description	Fruit description	Comments
Ceratonia siliqua, carob	Evergreen tree to 25' high, 15–20' wide. Deep green divided leaves with rounded leaflets. Grown for dark brown seedpods. Hardy to 20°F.	Dark brown, 12"-long seedpod is baked, ground, and used as chocolate substitute. Sweet.	Grown from seed or semihardwood cuttings. Pods may ferment on the tree in hot, humid climates. Not all trees are self-fruitful.
Chrysophyllum cainito, star apple, caimito	Attractive evergreen tree, usually to about 25' high and wide but can be taller. Glossy dark green leaves, silky bronze beneath. Hardy to 28–30°F.	Globe-shape; 4" diameter, green or purple, tough skin. Star-shape core has mild, grapelike interior, hard seed.	Best peeled and eaten fresh. Grown from seed.
Coffea arabica, coffee	Evergreen shrub or small tree, upright growth to 12' high, 4–6' wide. Handsome, deep green leaves, small, fragrant white flowers. Hardy to 32°F.	Oblong, smooth-skinned, ¾" diameter, red when ripe, contains two seeds, takes 7–9 months to ripen.	Seeds roasted to make coffee. Best in partial shade outdoors but also a popular houseplant. Grown from seed or semihardwood cuttings.
Cudrania tricuspidata (*Maclura tricuspidata*), che	Deciduous tree or large shrub, to 25' high and wide. Hardy to –20°F.	Round, like mulberry crossed with lychee, red to reddish purple, 1–2", sweet, juicy red flesh.	Tough, drought tolerant. Fruit tastes better than related mulberry, hints of watermelon. Usually grown from seed. Prune to control shape. Allow to ripen on tree.
Dovyalis caffra, kei apple	Evergreen shrub or small tree, 10–20' high, 10' wide, very thorny. Small greenish yellow flowers. Hardy to 20°F.	Round, 1" diameter, deep yellow-orange with juicy, aromatic yellow flesh. Tart until fully ripe.	Need male and female plants for pollination. Seedlings only 50% true to type; grow from semihardwood cuttings or select grafted plants.
Eugenia aggregata, cherry of the Rio Grande	Evergreen shrub, 10–15' high, 4–6' wide, peeling bark, white flowers. Hardy to 20°F.	Dark red, oblong fruit, 1" diameter, has cherry flavor.	Good for making pies. Usually grown from seed.
Eugenia brasiliensis, grumichama	Attractive small evergreen tree, 10–15' high, 6–8' wide. Small white flowers. Hardy to 27°F.	Round, ¾" diameter, purplish black skin, sweet, white flesh.	Unreliable from seed but easy from cuttings. Considered best *Eugenia* by many.
Eugenia luschnathiana, pitomba	Evergeen shrub, 10–15' high, 8–10' wide. Attractive foliage. Hardy to 27°F.	Round, 1½" diameter, bright yellow skin, white flesh, juicy, mildly acidic.	Usually grown from seed but quality unpredictable. Makes good jam.

Barbados cherry fruits are high in Vitamin C.

Jaboticaba fruits are borne directly on the stem.

Prickly pear fruits are yellow to purple when ripe.

Malabar chestnut has edible nuts inside a large fruit.

OTHER SUBTROPICAL FRUIT SPECIES *(continued)*

Species	Plant description	Fruit description	Comments
Eugenia uniflora, Surinam cherry, pitanga	Evergreen shrub or small tree, 10–15' high, 6–8' wide. Handsome foliage, small white flowers. Hardy to 30°F.	Round with 8 ribs, ¾" diameter, dark red to black, sweet-tart flavor.	Popular ornamental. Unreliable from seed but easily grown from cuttings. Select plants with quality fruit. Good for making jellies or jams. 'Lolita' and 'Vermillion' are superior fruiters.
Euphoria longan, longan	Evergreen tree, 25–40' high and equally wide. Upright clusters of yellowish white flowers. Hardy to 24°F.	Round, 1" diameter, grapelike clusters. Yellow to brown skin, sweet, white flesh.	Seedlings slow to bear fruit. Propagate by air layering. Related to lychee. 'Kohala' and 'Ship'i' are improved varieties.
Garcinia mangostana, mangosteen	Evergreen tree, 10–20' high by 8–12' wide. Large, yellow-red flowers. Hardy to 32°F.	Round, 3" diameter, thick dark reddish purple skin. Segmented, translucent, sweet flesh.	All plant parts produce yellow latex. Grow from seed or select grafted plants.
Hovenia dulcis, raisin tree	Deciduous tree, 15–25' high by 8–12' wide. Small, greenish purple flowers. Hardy to -10°F.	Grown for fleshy flower stems, which taste like raisins. Small brown fruit not used.	Usually grown from seed.
Macadamia spp., macadamia	Evergreen tree, 30–40' high and spreading at least as wide. Mature tree hardy to 24°F; flower clusters killed at 28°F.	Round, 1–1½" diameter, delicious creamy white nut with high oil content. Sweet.	'Arkin Papershell', 'Beaumont', 'Dana White', and 'Kaui' are good varieties in Florida. 'Beaumont', 'Burdick', 'Cate', 'Elimbah', and 'James' in California. 'Ikaika', 'Kakea', 'Kau', 'Keaau', 'Makai', 'Mauka', and 'Pahala' in Hawaii.
Malpighia glabra, acerola cherry, Barbados cherry	Evergreen to semideciduous shrub, 6–10' high by 4–6' wide. Small, white to pink flowers. Hardy to 30°F.	Round, 1" diameter, cherrylike, bright red, tinged yellow, sweet to acid. High in vitamin C. Fruit tends to drop in cool climates.	Tomato-set hormone sprays may increase yields. Propagate by hardwood or semihardwood cuttings. 'B-17', 'Florida Sweet' and 'Manoa Sweet' are improved varieties.
Manilkara zapota, sapodilla	Evergreen tree, 20–40' high by 15–30' wide. Small, green to brown flowers are fragrant at night. Hardy to 28°F	Oval 2–4" diameter, gray to brown, with sweet translucent yellowish flesh.	Milky sap used to flavor chewing gum. Can be grown from seed, but 'Alano', 'Hasya', 'Makok', 'Molix', and 'Morena' are improved selections.
Myrciaria cauliflora, jaboticaba	Evergreen tree, 15–30' high by 8–12' wide. Small, white flowers produced directly on bark. Hardy to 25°F.	Round, 1" diameter, borne on small branches and trunk, purplish black skin, translucent white flesh, grapelike, juicy.	Unusual fruiting habit. Seedlings fruit in about 8 years. Can be air layered.
Opuntia ficus-indica, prickly pear	Evergreen, mostly thornless cactus, upright growth to 7–15' high. Attractive yellow flowers. Hardy to 26°F.	Oval, 3–4" diameter, yellow to reddish purple skin, red flesh, slightly tart.	Handle fruit carefully, skin covered with spines. Easy to propagate by rooting small padlike branches.

Canistel fruits resemble teardrop-shape eggs.

Capulin cherry turns deep purple when ripe.

Sugarcane is a member of the grass family.

'So' jujube bears round brownish fruits.

OTHER SUBTROPICAL FRUIT SPECIES *(continued)*

Species	Plant description	Fruit description	Comments
Pachira aquatica, (*Bombax glabra*) Malabar chestnut	Evergreen shrub or small tree, 10–15' high, 8–10' feet wide. Large fragrant greenish white to pink and red flowers. Hardy to 28°F.	Large, round, 4–12" diameter brown fruit contains several ½" diameter, edible nuts with peanutlike flavor.	Fruit splits open when ripe, seeds may fall out. Edible raw or roasted. Grown from seed.
Pouteria campechiana, canistel, eggfruit	Evergreen tree to at least 20–25' high. Long bright green leaves, small creamy white flowers. Mature tree hardy to 23°F, young tree to 29°F.	Oblong to round, 3–5' long, 2–3" wide, bright yellow to orange, firm creamy flesh like a hard-boiled egg. Musky baked sweet potato flavor.	Self-fruitful. May fruit twice a year. Drought tolerant. Propagated by seed, grafting, or budding. 'Fairchild #1', 'Fitzpatrick', 'Oro', and 'Trompo' are improved varieties.
Prunus salicifolia, capulin cherry	Evergreen to semideciduous tree, very fast growing, 20–30' high, 10–20' wide. Shiny foliage, fragrant white flowers. Hardy to 20°F.	Round, 1" diameter, cherrylike, dark purple skin, green flesh. Good quality, sweet-tart flavor.	Very low chilling requirement. Will set fruit in 3 or 4 years from seed, but quality is variable. Can be air layered. Self-fruitful. Superior selections, such as 'Lomeli' and 'Werner', sometimes available.
Saccharum officinarum, sugarcane	Evergreen perennial, upright growth 6–10' high. Forms spreading clump. Shoots hardy to 32°F, roots slightly hardier.	Grown for sweet thick green or purple canes.	Highest sugar content in midsummer to late fall. Will root at stem nodes. Can also be propagated by root division.
Synsepalum dulcificum, miracle fruit	Evergreen shrub, 6–10' high, 3–6' wide. Small white flower clusters. Hardy to 32°F.	Oval, ¾" diameter, red, succulent flesh.	Sour flavors taste sweet after eating miracle fruit. Propagate by seed, semihardwood cuttings, or air layering.
Syzygium jambos, rose apple	Evergreen large shrub or small tree, to 20' high. Handsome narrow leaves, shiny pink when new, turning dull green. Large (2–4") showy fragrant white flowers in spring. Hardy to 25°F.	Flattened sphere, 1–2" in diameter, green to yellow-pink, crisp with sweet, rose-scented flesh. Seeds poisonous.	Propagated by seed or semihardwood cuttings.
Tamarindus indica, tamarind	Evergreen tree, 20–40' high, at least as wide. Small clusters of yellow-red flowers. Hardy to 26°F.	Pods 5" long, reddish brown, edible flesh surrounding small hard seeds. Sweet-tart flavor.	Usually grown from seed. Can be grown from semihardwood and softwood cuttings. Young trees are cold sensitive.
Ziziphus jujuba, jujube	Deciduous tree, 20–25' high, 15–20' wide, gnarled branches. Clusters of small yellow flowers. Hardy to –20°F.	Round to oval, ¾–1" diameter, light green to reddish brown, apple flavor.	Good for hot or cold climates. Can be eaten crisp or dried. Grow from seed or by air layering. 'Li' and 'Lang' are most common selections.

RESOURCES

Information
Your state cooperative extension service is also a good source of information.

Association of Tropical Fruit Growers
userwww.sfsu.edu/~msuen
/DAI527/05/fruits.html

California Rare Fruit Growers
66 Farragut Ave.
San Francisco, CA 94112-4050
crfg.org

Desert Tropicals
desert-tropicals.com

Echonet
echonet.org/eln&herbs
/eln_catalog/fruittreesA.htm

North American Fruit Explorers
1716 Apples Rd.
Chapin, IL 62628
217/245-7589
nafex.org

Purdue University Center for New Crops and Plant Products
hort.purdue.edu/newcrop

Rare Fruit Council International
14735 S.W. 48 Terr.
Miami, FL 33185
305/554-1333

Rare Fruit Internet Forum
rarefruit@yahoogroups.com

Texas Citrus and Subtropical Fruits
aggie-horticulture.tamu.edu
/citrus/urban.htm

University of California
Fruit and Nut Research and Information Center
fruitsandnuts.ucdavis.edu

University of California, Riverside
Citrus Variety Collection
citrusvariety.ucr.edu

University of Florida FruitScapes
fruitscapes.ifas.ufl.edu

We Be Bananas
webebananas.com

Mail-order subtropical fruit sources
State regulations often prevent shipments between states. Check with the nursery to find out about restrictions.

Aloha Tropicals
P.O. Box 6042
Oceanside, CA 92052
760/631-2880
alohatropicals.com

Bamboo Plantation
642 Columbine Ln. SW
Brookhaven, MS 39601
601/833-3937
www.bambooplantation.com

Bay Laurel Nursery
2500 El Camino Real
Atascadero, CA 93422
805/466-3406
baylaurelnursery.com

Excalibur Rare Fruit Trees
5200 Fearnley Rd.
Lake Worth, FL 33467–5650
561/969-6988
excaliburfruittrees.com

Exotica Nursery
2508-B E. Vista Way
Vista, CA 92083
760/724-9093

Four Winds Growers
www.fourwindsgrowers.com

Fruit Lover's Nursery
P.O. Box 1597
Pahoa, HI 96778
808/965-0835
fruitlovers.com

Garden of Delights
14560 S.W. 14th St.
Davie, FL 33325–4217
800/741-3103
gardenofdelights.com

Going Bananas
24401 S.W. 197 Ave.
Homestead, FL 33031
305/247-0397
going-bananas.com

Greenearth Publishing
P.O. Box 243
Melbourne, FL 32902
800/927-3084
greenhousebusiness.com

Hidden Springs Nursery
170 Hidden Springs Ln.
Cookeville, TN 38501
931/268-2592
hiddenspringsnursery.com

J. D. Andersen Nursery
2790 Marvinga Ln.
Fallbrook, CA 92028
760/723-2907
jdandersen.com

Jené's Tropicals
6831 Central Ave.
St. Petersburg, FL 33710
727/344-1668
tropicalfruit.com

Just Fruits and Exotics
30 St. Frances St.
Crawfordville, FL 32327
850/926-5644
justfruitsandexotics.com

Pacific Tropical Gardens
16-410 Orchidland Dr.
P.O. Box 5861
Hilo, HI 96720
808/896-6183
pctgardens.com

Papaya Tree Nursery
12422 El Oro Way
Granada Hills, CA 91344
818/363-3680
papayatreenursery.com

Pine Island Nursery
16300 S.W. 184th St.
Miami, FL 33187
305/233-5501
tropicalfruitnursery.com

Possum Trot Tropical Fruit Nursery
14955 S.W. 214th St.
Miami, FL 33187
305/235-1768

Raintree Nursery
391 Butts Rd.
Morton, WA 98356
360/496-6400
raintreenursery.com

The Nursery at TyTy
4723 U.S. Hwy. 82 W
P.O. Box 130
TyTy, GA 31795
800/972-2101
tytyga.com

INDEX

Note: Page references in **bold type** refer to Gallery entries and include photographs. Page references in *italic type* refer to additional photographs, illustrations, and information in captions. Plants are listed by their common names.

A

Acerola or Barbados cherry *(Malpighia glabra)*, 116, **120**
Acidic soils, 22
Adaptation to cold climates, 35
  USDA Plant Hardiness Zones, 9, *9*
  See also Climate; Frost protection; *under specific fruits*
Advective freeze, defined, 14
Aeration. *See* Soil drainage/ aeration
Alkaline soils, 22
Alligator pear. *See* Avocado
Animal pests, 27
Anthracnose (fungal leaf spots), 27
Antitranspirant sprays, *15*
Ants, aphids and, 25
Aphids, 25, *25*
Atemoya *(Annona* hybrid), **76**
Avocado, alligator pear, or love fruit *(Persea americana)*, **64–69**
  adaptation, 6, 64–65
  caring for, 23, 67–68
  culinary uses, 69
  dwarf varieties, 69
  harvest and storage, *64*, 68–69, *69*
  insect pests, *26*
  landscape uses, 66–67
  pollination, 65
  propagation, 66
  site selection and planting, 66
  varieties for California, 65
  varieties for Florida, 67
  varieties for Hawaii, 68

B

Banana or plantain *(Musa acuminata* and *M. balbisiana)*, **70–73**
  adaptation, 35, 70
  caring for, 71
  culinary uses, 72
  harvest and storage, 72, *72*
  heat requirement, 9
  landscape uses, 7, *33*, 36, 71, *71*
  pollination, 70–71
  propagation, 28, 31, 71
  site selection and planting, 71
  varieties, 72–73
  wind damage, *10*
Barbados or acerola cherry *(Malpighia glabra)*, 116, **120,** *120*
Bare-root plants, 17, *17*, 20
Basin irrigation, 21
Birds, as pests, 27, *27*
Boron deficiency, 22
Budding, *29*, 30, *30*, 42

C

Caimito or star apple *(Chrysophyllum cainito)*, 118, **119**
Callus, defined, 29
Cambium, defined, 29
Canistel or eggfruit *(Pouteria campechiana)*, **121,** *121*
Capulin cherry *(Prunus salicifolia)*, **121,** *121*
Carambola or starfruit *(Averrhoa carambola)*, **116**
Carob *(Ceratonia siliqua)*, **119**
Caterpillars, 25, *25*
Che *(Cudrania tricuspidata)*, **119,** *119*
Cherimoya *(Annona cherimola)*, **74–77**
  adaptation, 8, 9, 74–75
  caring for, 75–76
  culinary uses, 76
  harvest and storage, 76
  landscape uses, 75
  pollination, 74–75
  relatives, 76
  site selection and planting, 75
  varieties, 77
Cherry of the Rio Grande *(Eugenia aggregata)*, **119**
Chilling requirements, 10, 28
Chinese gooseberry. *See* Kiwifruit
Choosing plants, 17, *17*
Citrange, rootstocks, 42
Citron *(Citrus medica)*, **46**
Citrumelo, 'Swingle' rootstocks, 42
Citrus
  adaptation, 6, *8*, 11, *13*, 35, 40, 46
  benefits of growing, *38*, 39
  caring for, 43, 44, 46
  climate effects, 41
  for containers, 36, *37*, 43, 46
  diversity, 39, *40, 41*
  dwarfing rootstocks, 42
  frost protection, *14–15*
  growing regions, *39*
  harvest and storage, *42*, 45, 46
  history, 39
  as indoor plants, *33*, 36
  insect pests, 25, 26, *26*
  landscape uses, *4*, 43, *43*, 46
  overview, 46
  pollination, 42
  propagation, 28, *28*, 29, 42, 46
  pruning and training, 24, *24*
  resources, *17*, 122
  rootstocks, 42
  site selection and planting, 43
  types of, **46–61**
  See also specific types of citrus
Clayey soils, 18, 22
Climate
  chilling requirement, 10
  cold tolerance, *8*, 9, *9*, 39
  heat requirement, 9
  USDA Plant Hardiness Zones, 9, *9*
  watering and, 21
  wind, 10
  See also adaptation under specific fruits; Humidity; Microclimates; Rainfall
Climate regions, 11, 12
Coffee *(Coffea arabica)*, 118, **119**
Cold tolerance. *See* Adaptation to cold climates
Container gardens
  bananas for, 7, *71*
  benefits, 18, 32, *32, 33*
  best subtropical fruits for, 36–37
  citrus for, 6, 43, 46
  dwarf avocados for, 69
  fertilizing, 34, *34*
  for frost protection, 12, 14, *15*, 32, 35, *35*
  how to move, 37
  passionfruit for, *106*
  planting, 17
  root pruning, 34
  soils for, 33
  watering, 34
Container-grown plants, *17, 19*
Containers, selecting, 33
Copper deficiency, 22

METRIC CONVERSIONS

U.S. UNITS TO METRIC EQUIVALENTS			METRIC EQUIVALENTS TO U.S. UNITS		
To Convert From	Multiply by	To Get	To Convert From	Multiply by	To Get
Inches	25.4	Millimeters	Millimeters	0.0394	Inches
Inches	2.54	Centimeters	Centimeters	0.3937	Inches
Feet	30.48	Centimeters	Centimeters	0.0328	Feet
Feet	0.3048	Meters	Meters	3.2808	Feet
Yards	0.9144	Meters	Meters	1.0936	Yards
Square inches	6.4516	Square centimeters	Square centimeters	0.1550	Square inches
Square feet	0.0929	Square meters	Square meters	10.764	Square feet
Square yards	0.8361	Square meters	Square meters	1.1960	Square yards
Acres	0.4047	Hectares	Hectares	2.4711	Acres
Cubic inches	16.387	Cubic centimeters	Cubic centimeters	0.0610	Cubic inches
Cubic feet	0.0283	Cubic meters	Cubic meters	35.315	Cubic feet
Cubic feet	28.316	Liters	Liters	0.0353	Cubic feet
Cubic yards	0.7646	Cubic meters	Cubic meters	1.308	Cubic yards
Cubic yards	764.55	Liters	Liters	0.0013	Cubic yards

To convert from degrees Fahrenheit (F) to degrees Celsius (C), first subtract 32, then multiply by ⁵⁄₉.

To convert from degrees Celsius to degrees Fahrenheit, multiply by ⁹⁄₅, then add 32.

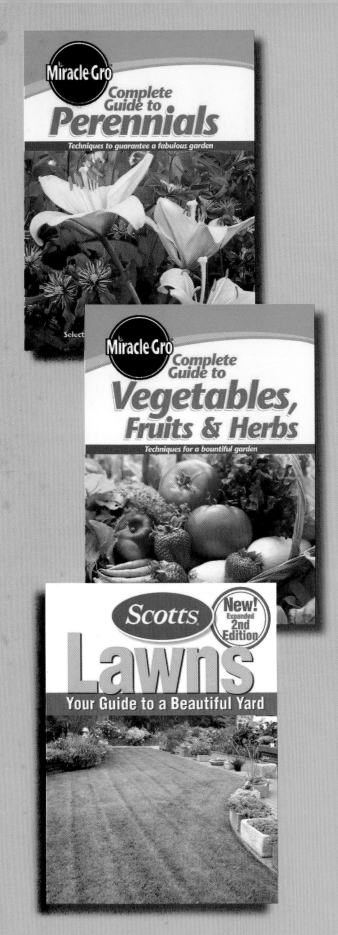